B

First Published	1970
Seventh Edition	2018
Eight Edition	2020

ISBN 978-983-2218-37-1

bpt@bahai.org.my

BAHÁ'Í PUBLISHING TRUST
OF MALAYSIA

BAHÁ'Í PRAYERS

Revealed by Bahá'u'lláh, the Báb and 'Abdu'l-Bahá
A selection for all occasions

Blessed is the spot, and the house,
and the place, and the city,
and the heart, and the mountain,
and the refuge, and the cave,
and the valley, and the land,
and the sea, and the island,
and the meadow where mention
of God hath been made,
and His praise glorified.

—Bahá'u'lláh,

O God, my God, my Beloved,
my heart's Desire.

—The Báb

CONTENTS

The headings listed here are purely arbitrary for ease of reference and are not a part of the authentic text.

Bahá'i Prayers

Occasional Prayers and Special Tablets

Intone, O My servant, the verses of God
that have been received by thee,
as intoned by them who have drawn
nigh unto Him,
that the sweetness of thy melody
may kindle thine own soul,
and attract the hearts of all men.
Whoso reciteth, in the privacy of his chamber,
the verses revealed by God,
the scattering angels of the Almighty
shall scatter abroad the fragrance
of the words uttered by his mouth,
and shall cause the heart
of every righteous man to throb.
Though he may, at first, remain unaware
of its effect, yet the virtue of the grace
vouchsafed unto him must needs
sooner or later exercise its influence
upon his soul.
Thus have the mysteries of the Revelation of God
been decreed by virtue of the Will of Him
Who is the Source of power and wisdom.

—Bahá'u'lláh

Recite ye the verses of God every morn and eventide. Whoso faileth to recite them hath not been faithful to the Covenant of God and His Testament, and whoso turneth away from these holy verses in this Day is of those who throughout eternity have turned away from God.

Fear ye God, O My servants, one and all. Pride not yourselves on much reading of the verses or on a multitude of pious acts by night and day; for were a man to read a single verse with joy and radiance it would be better for him than to read with lassitude all the Holy Books of God, the Help in Peril, the Self-Subsisting.

—Bahá'u'lláh, Kitáb-i-Aqdas

Immerse yourselves in the ocean of My words, that ye may unravel its secrets, and discover all the pearls of wisdom that lie hid in its depths. Take heed that ye do not vacillate in your determination to embrace the truth of this Cause—a Cause through which the potentialities of the might of God have been revealed, and His sovereignty established.

—Bahá'u'lláh

OBLIGATORY PRAYERS

GUIDANCE ON OBLIGATORY PRAYERS

Bahá'u'lláh has revealed three Obligatory Prayers. The believer is entirely free to choose any one of these three prayers, but is under the obligation of reciting one of them, and in accordance with any specific directions with which it may be accompanied. They should be said individually but are not dependent on a private spot.

Performing ablutions, (which are washing the hands and face in preparation for prayer), and facing in the direction of the Qiblih (the Point of Adoration, the Most Holy Tomb is at Bahji, Akká), are fixed requirements for the recitation of the Obligatory Prayers. Ablutions are essential whether a bath has been taken previously or not.

"By 'morning,' 'noon' and 'evening,' mentioned in connection with the Obligatory Prayers, is meant respectively the intervals between sunrise and noon, between noon and sunset, and from sunset till two hours after sunset."

—Synopsis & Codification of Kitáb-i-Aqdas

"These daily Obligatory Prayers, ...together with a few other specific ones, such as the Healing Prayer, the Tablet of Ahmad, have been invested by Bahá'u'lláh with a special potency and significance, and should therefore be accepted as such and be recited by the believers with unquestioning faith and confidence, that through them they may enter into a much closer communion with God, and identify themselves more fully with His laws and precepts." —Directives from Shoghi Effendi.

EXEMPTION

Exemption from offering the Obligatory Prayers and fasting is granted to those who are ill, those who are over 70 and women in their courses.

For women in their courses:
Let them, instead, after performance of their ablutions, give praise unto God, repeating ninety-five times between the noon of one day and the next

"*Glorified be God, the Lord of Splendor and Beauty.*"

When traveling, if ye should stop and rest in some safe spot, perform ye – men and women alike – a single prostration in place of each unsaid Obligatory Prayer, and while prostrating say

"*Glorified be God, the Lord of Might and Majesty, of Grace and Bounty.*"

Whoso is unable to do this, let him say only

"*Glorified be God*";

this shall assuredly suffice him. He is, of a truth, the all-sufficing, the ever-abiding, the forgiving, compassionate God. Upon completing your prostrations, seat yourselves cross-legged – men and women alike – and eighteen times repeat

"*Glorified be God, the Lord of the kingdoms of earth and heaven.*"

Let him that **findeth no water for ablution** repeat five times the words

"*In the Name of God, the Most Pure, the Most Pure,*" and then proceed to his devotions."

—Bahá'u'lláh, Kitáb-i-Aqdas

SHORT OBLIGATORY PRAYER

To be recited once a day between noon and sunset

I bear witness, O my God, that Thou hast created me to know Thee and to worship Thee.

I testify, at this moment, to my powerlessness and to Thy might, to my poverty and to Thy wealth. There is none other God but Thee, the Help in Peril, the Self-Subsisting.

—Bahá'u'lláh

"Fasting and obligatory prayer are as two wings to man's life. Blessed be the one who soareth with their aid in the heaven of the love of God,...." —Bahá'u'lláh

"in every word and movement of the Obligatory Prayer there are allusions, mysteries and a wisdom that man is unable to comprehend, and letters and scrolls cannot contain." —'Abdu'l-Bahá

MEDIUM OBLIGATORY PRAYER

To be recited daily, in the morning, at noon, and in the evening. Whoso wisheth to pray, let him wash his hands, and while he washeth, let him say:

Strengthen my hand, O my God, that it may take hold of Thy Book with such steadfastness that the hosts of the world shall have no power over it. Guard it, then, from meddling with whatsoever doth not belong unto it. Thou art, verily, the Almighty, the Most Powerful.

And while washing his face, let him say:

I have turned my face unto Thee, O my Lord! Illumine it with the light of Thy countenance. Protect it, then, from turning to any one but Thee.

Then let him stand up, and facing the Qiblih (Point of Adoration, i.e. Bahjí, 'Akká), let him say:

God testifieth that there is none other God but Him. His are the kingdoms of Revelation and of creation. He, in truth, hath manifested Him Who is the Dayspring of Revelation, Who conversed on Sinai, through Whom the Supreme Horizon hath been made to shine, and the Lote-Tree beyond which there is no passing hath spoken, and through Whom the call hath been proclaimed unto all who are in heaven and on earth: "Lo, the All-Possessing is come. Earth and heaven, glory and dominion are God's, the Lord of all men, and the Possessor of the Throne on high and of earth below!"

Let him, then, bend down, with hands resting on the knees, and say:

Exalted art Thou above my praise and the praise of anyone beside me, above my description and the description of all who are in heaven and all who are on earth!

Then, standing with open hands, palms upward toward the face, let him say:

Disappoint not, O my God, him that hath, with beseeching fingers, clung to the hem of Thy mercy and Thy grace, O Thou Who of those who show mercy art the Most Merciful!

Let him, then, be seated and say:

I bear witness to Thy unity and Thy oneness, and that Thou art God, and that there is none other God beside Thee. Thou hast, verily, revealed Thy Cause, fulfilled Thy Covenant, and opened wide the door of Thy grace to all that dwell in heaven and on earth. Blessing and peace, salutation and glory, rest upon Thy loved ones, whom the changes and chances of the world have not deterred from turning unto Thee, and who have given their all, in the hope of obtaining that which is with Thee. Thou art, in truth, the Ever-Forgiving, the All-Bountiful.

If anyone choose to recite instead of the long verse these words:

"God testifieth that there is none other God but Him, the Help in Peril, the Self-Subsisting,"

It would be sufficient. And likewise, it would suffice were he, while seated, to choose to recite these words:

"I bear witness to Thy unity and Thy oneness, and that Thou art God, and that there is none other God beside Thee." —Bahá'u'lláh

LONG OBLIGATORY PRAYER

To be recited once in twenty-four hours

Whoso wisheth to recite this prayer, let him stand up and turn unto God, and, as he standeth in his place, let him gaze to the right and to the left, as if awaiting the mercy of his Lord, the Most Merciful, the Compassionate. Then let him say:

O Thou Who art the Lord of all names and the Maker of the heavens! I beseech Thee by them Who are the Daysprings of Thine invisible Essence, the Most Exalted, the All-Glorious, to make of my prayer a fire that will burn away the veils which have shut me out from Thy beauty, and a light that will lead me unto the ocean of Thy Presence.

Let him then raise his hands in supplication toward God — blessed and exalted be He — and say:

O Thou the Desire of the world and the Beloved of the nations! Thou seest me turning toward Thee, and rid of all attachment to anyone save Thee, and clinging to Thy cord, through whose movement the whole creation hath been stirred up. I am Thy servant, O my Lord, and the son of Thy servant. Behold me standing ready to do Thy will and Thy desire, and wishing naught else except Thy good pleasure. I implore Thee by the Ocean of Thy mercy and the Day-Star of Thy grace to do with Thy servant as Thou willest and pleasest. By Thy might which is far above all mention and praise! Whatsoever is revealed by Thee is the desire of my heart and the beloved of my soul. O God, my God! Look not upon my hopes and my doings, nay rather look upon Thy will that hath encompassed the heavens and the earth. By Thy Most Great Name, O Thou Lord of all nations! I have desired only what Thou didst desire, and love only what Thou dost love.

Let him then kneel, and bowing his forehead to the ground, let him say:

Exalted art Thou above the description of anyone save Thyself, and the comprehension of aught else except Thee.

Let him then stand and say:

Make my prayer, O my Lord, a fountain of living waters whereby I may live as long as Thy sovereignty endureth, and may make mention of Thee in every world of Thy worlds.

Let him again raise his hands in supplication, and say:

O Thou in separation from Whom hearts and souls have melted, and by the fire of Whose love the whole world hath been set aflame! I implore Thee by Thy Name through which Thou hast subdued the whole creation, not to withhold from me that which is with Thee, O Thou Who rulest over all men! Thou seest, O my Lord, this stranger hastening to his most exalted home beneath the canopy of Thy majesty and within the precincts of Thy mercy; and this transgressor seeking the ocean of Thy forgiveness; and this lowly one the court of Thy glory; and this poor creature the orient of Thy wealth. Thine is the authority to command whatsoever Thou willest. I bear witness that Thou art to be praised in Thy doings, and to be obeyed in Thy behests, and to remain unconstrained in Thy bidding.

Let him then raise his hands, and repeat three times the Greatest Name (Alláh-u-Abhá). Let him then bend down with hands resting on the knees before God — blessed and exalted be He — and say:

Thou seest, O my God, how my spirit hath been stirred up within my limbs and members, in its longing to worship Thee, and in its yearning to remember Thee and extol Thee; how it testifieth to that whereunto the Tongue of Thy Commandment hath testified in the kingdom of Thine utterance and the heaven of Thy knowledge. I love, in this state, O my Lord, to beg of Thee all that is with Thee, that I may demonstrate my poverty, and magnify Thy bounty and Thy riches, and may declare my powerlessness, and manifest Thy power and Thy might.

Let him then stand and raise his hands twice in supplication, and say:

There is no God but Thee, the Almighty, the All-Bountiful. There is no God but Thee, the Ordainer, both in the beginning and in the end. O God, my God! Thy forgiveness hath emboldened me, and Thy mercy hath strengthened me, and Thy call hath awakened me, and Thy grace hath raised me up and led me unto Thee. Who, otherwise, am I that I should dare to stand at the gate of the city of Thy nearness, or set my face toward the lights that are shining from the heaven of Thy will? Thou seest, O my Lord, this wretched creature knocking at the door of Thy grace, and this evanescent soul seeking the river of everlasting life from the hands of Thy bounty. Thine is the command at all times, O Thou Who art the Lord of all names; and mine is resignation and willing submission to Thy will, O Creator of the heavens!

Let him then raise his hands thrice, and say: [1]

Greater is God than every great one!

---

1 "The hands should be raised three times and each time the sentence be repeated in conjunction with the act."
—Universal House of Justice, Lights of Guidance 1534

Let him then kneel and, bowing his forehead to the ground, say:

Too high art Thou for the praise of those who are nigh unto Thee to ascend unto the heaven of Thy nearness, or for the birds of the hearts of them who are devoted to Thee to attain to the door of Thy gate. I testify that Thou hast been sanctified above all attributes and holy above all names. No God is there but Thee, the Most Exalted, the All-Glorious.

Let him then seat himself and say:

I testify unto that whereunto have testified all created things, and the Concourse on high, and the inmates of the all-highest Paradise, and beyond them the Tongue of Grandeur itself from the all-glorious Horizon, that Thou art God, that there is no God but Thee, and that He Who hath been manifested is the Hidden Mystery, the Treasured Symbol, through Whom the letters B and E (Be) have been joined and knit together. I testify that it is He whose name hath been set down by the Pen of the Most High, and Who hath been mentioned in the Books of God, the Lord of the Throne on high and of earth below.

Let him then stand erect and say:

O Lord of all being and Possessor of all things visible and invisible! Thou dost perceive my tears and the sighs I utter, and hearest my groaning, and my wailing, and the lamentation of my heart. By Thy might! My trespasses have kept me back from drawing nigh unto Thee; and my sins have held me far from the court of Thy holiness. Thy love, O my Lord, hath enriched me, and separation from Thee hath destroyed me, and remoteness from Thee hath consumed me. I entreat Thee by Thy footsteps in this wilderness, and by the words "Here am I. Here am I" which Thy chosen Ones have uttered in this immensity, and by the breaths of Thy Revelation, and the gentle winds of the Dawn of Thy Manifestation, to ordain that I may gaze on Thy beauty and observe whatsoever is in Thy Book.

Let him then repeat the Greatest Name thrice, and bend down with hands resting on the knees, and say:

Praise be to Thee, O my God, that Thou hast aided me to remember Thee and to praise Thee, and hast made known unto me Him Who is the Dayspring of Thy signs, and hast caused me to bow down before Thy Lordship, and humble myself before Thy Godhead, and to acknowledge that which hath been uttered by the Tongue of Thy grandeur.

Let him then rise and say:

O God, my God! My back is bowed by the burden of my sins, and my heedlessness hath destroyed me. Whenever I ponder my evil doings and Thy benevolence, my heart melteth within me, and my blood boileth in my veins. By Thy Beauty, O Thou the Desire of the world! I blush to lift up my face to Thee, and my longing hands are ashamed to stretch forth toward the heaven of Thy bounty. Thou seest, O my God, how my tears prevent me from remembering Thee and from extolling Thy virtues, O Thou the Lord of the Throne on high and of earth below!

I implore Thee by the signs of Thy Kingdom and the mysteries of Thy Dominion to do with Thy loved ones as becometh Thy bounty, O Lord of all being, and is worthy of Thy grace, O King of the seen and the unseen!

Let him then repeat the Greatest Name thrice, and kneel with his forehead to the ground, and say:

Praise be unto Thee, O our God, that Thou hast sent down unto us that which draweth us nigh unto Thee, and supplieth us with every good thing sent down by Thee in Thy Books and Thy Scriptures. Protect us, we beseech Thee, O my Lord, from the hosts of idle fancies and vain imaginations. Thou, in truth, art the Mighty, the All-Knowing.

Let him then raise his head, and seat himself, and say:

I testify, O my God, to that whereunto Thy chosen Ones have testified, and acknowledge that which the inmates of the all-highest Paradise and those who have circled round Thy mighty Throne have acknowledged. The kingdoms of earth and heaven are Thine, O Lord of the worlds!

—Bahá'u'lláh, Kitáb-i-Aqdas

RECITATION OF THE GREATEST NAME

NINETY-FIVE TIMES

Alláh-u-Abhá

God the All-Glorious

It hath been ordained that every believer in God, the Lord of Judgement, shall, each day, having washed his hands and then his face, seat himself and, turning unto God, repeat "Alláh-u-Abhá" ninety-five times.

Such was the decree of the Maker of the Heavens when, with majesty and power, He established Himself upon the thrones of His Names. —Bahá'u'lláh, Kitáb-i-Aqdas

AID & ASSISTANCE

"He, verily, will assist thee with the hosts of the seen and unseen..."

—Bahá'u'lláh

O my God! I ask Thee, by Thy most glorious Name, to aid me in that which will cause the affairs of Thy servants to prosper, and Thy cities to flourish. Thou, indeed, hast power over all things!

—Bahá'u'lláh

O Thou Whose face is the object of my adoration, Whose beauty is my sanctuary, Whose habitation is my goal, Whose praise is my hope, Whose providence is my companion, Whose love is the cause of my being, Whose mention is my solace, Whose nearness is my desire, Whose presence is my dearest wish and highest aspiration, I entreat Thee not to withhold from me the things Thou didst ordain for the chosen ones among Thy servants.

Supply me, then, with the good of this world and of the next. Thou, truly, art the King of all men. There is no God but Thee, the Ever-Forgiving, the Most Generous.

—Bahá'u'lláh

Is there any Remover of difficulties save God? Say: Praised be God! He is God! All are His servants, and all abide by His bidding!

—The Báb

Say: God sufficeth all things above all things, and nothing in the heavens or in the earth but God sufficeth. Verily, He is in Himself the Knower, the Sustainer, the Omnipotent.

—The Báb

Lord! Pitiful are we, grant us Thy favor; poor, bestow upon us a share from the ocean of Thy wealth; needy, do Thou satisfy us; abased, give us Thy glory. The fowls of the air and the beasts of the field receive their meat each day from Thee, and all beings partake of Thy care and loving-kindness. Deprive not this feeble one of Thy wondrous grace and vouchsafe by Thy might unto this helpless soul Thy bounty. Give us our daily bread, and grant Thine increase in the necessities of life, that we may be dependent on none other but Thee, may commune wholly with Thee, may walk in Thy ways and declare Thy mysteries. Thou art the Almighty and the Loving and the Provider of all mankind.

—'Abdu'l-Bahá

O Lord my God! Assist Thy loved ones to be firm in Thy Faith, to walk in Thy ways, to be steadfast in Thy Cause. Give them Thy grace to withstand the onslaught of self and passion, to follow the light of divine guidance. Thou art the Powerful, the Gracious, the Self-Subsisting, the Bestower, the Compassionate, the Almighty, the All-Bountiful.

—'Abdu'l-Bahá

PRAYER FOR NATURAL PHENOMENA

"On the appearance of fearful natural events (which cause alarm such as earthquakes) call ye to mind the might and majesty of your Lord, He Who heareth and seeth all, and say

Dominion is God's, the Lord of the seen and the unseen, the Lord of creation."

—Bahá'u'lláh, Kitáb-i-Aqdas

CHILDREN

INFANTS

Praised be Thou, O Lord my God! Graciously grant that this infant be fed from the breast of Thy tender mercy and loving providence and be nourished with the fruit of Thy celestial trees. Suffer him not to be committed to the care of anyone save Thee, inasmuch as Thou, Thyself, through the potency of Thy sovereign will and power, didst create and call him into being. There is none other God but Thee, the Almighty, the All-Knowing.

Lauded art Thou, O my Best Beloved, waft over him the sweet savors of Thy transcendent bounty and the fragrances of Thy holy bestowals. Enable him then to seek shelter beneath the shadow of Thy most exalted Name, O Thou Who holdest in Thy grasp the kingdom of names and attributes. Verily, Thou art potent to do what Thou willest, and Thou art indeed the Mighty, the Exalted, the Ever-Forgiving, the Gracious, the Generous, the Merciful.

—Bahá'u'lláh

O God! Rear this little babe in the bosom of Thy love, and give it milk from the breast of Thy Providence. Cultivate this fresh plant in the rose garden of Thy love and aid it to grow through the showers of Thy bounty. Make it a child of the kingdom, and lead it to Thy heavenly realm. Thou art powerful and kind, and Thou art the Bestower, the Generous, the Lord of surpassing bounty.

—'Abdu'l-Bahá

CHILDREN

O Lord! Make these children excellent plants. Let them grow and develop in the Garden of Thy Covenant, and bestow freshness and beauty through the outpourings of the clouds of the Abhá Kingdom.

O Thou kind Lord! I am a little child, exalt me by admitting me to the kingdom. I am earthly, make me heavenly; I am of the world below, let me belong to the realm above; gloomy, suffer me to become radiant; material, make me spiritual, and grant that I may manifest Thine infinite bounties. Thou art the Powerful, the All-Loving. —'Abdu'l-Bahá

O God! Educate these children. These children are the plants of Thine orchard, the flowers of Thy meadow, the roses of Thy garden. Let Thy rain fall upon them; let the Sun of Reality shine upon them with Thy love. Let Thy breeze refresh them in order that they may be trained, grow and develop, and appear in the utmost beauty. Thou art the Giver. Thou art the Compassionate.

—'Abdu'l-Bahá

O Thou kind Lord! These lovely children are the handiwork of the fingers of Thy might and the wondrous signs of Thy greatness. O God! Protect these children, graciously assist them to be educated and enable them to render service to the world of humanity. O God! These children are pearls, cause them to be nurtured within the shell of Thy loving-kindness. Thou art the Bountiful, the All-Loving.

—'Abdu'l-Bahá

O God, guide me, protect me, make of me a shining lamp and a brilliant star. Thou art the Mighty and the Powerful.

—'Abdu'l-Bahá

O my Lord! O my Lord! I am a child of tender years. Nourish me from the breast of Thy mercy, train me in the bosom of Thy love, educate me in the school of Thy guidance and develop me under the shadow of Thy bounty. Deliver me from darkness, make me a brilliant light; free me from unhappiness, make me a flower of the rose garden; suffer me to become a servant of Thy threshold and confer upon me the disposition and nature of the righteous; make me a cause of bounty to the human world, and crown my head with the diadem of eternal life. Verily, Thou art the Powerful, the Mighty, the Seer, the Hearer.

—'Abdu'l-Bahá

O Thou most glorious Lord! Make this little maidservant of Thine blessed and happy; cause her to be cherished at the threshold of Thy oneness and let her drink deep from the cup of Thy love so that she may be filled with rapture and ecstasy and diffuse sweet-scented fragrance. Thou art the Mighty and the Powerful, and Thou art the All-Knowing, the All-Seeing.

—'Abdu'l-Bahá

DETACHMENT

O Lord! Unto Thee I repair for refuge, and toward all Thy signs I set my heart. O Lord! Whether traveling or at home, and in my occupation or in my work, I place my whole trust in Thee. Grant me then Thy sufficing help so as to make me independent of all things, O Thou Who art unsurpassed in Thy mercy! Bestow upon me my portion, O Lord, as Thou pleasest, and cause me to be satisfied with whatsoever thou hast ordained for me. Thine is the absolute authority to command.

—The Báb

O my God, my Lord and my Master! I have detached myself from my kindred and have sought through Thee to become independent of all that dwell on earth and ever ready to receive that which is praiseworthy in Thy sight. Bestow on me such good as will make me independent of aught else but Thee, and grant me an ampler share of Thy boundless favors. Verily, Thou art the Lord of grace abounding.

—The Báb

O God! My God! Thou art my Hope and my Beloved, my highest Aim and Desire! With great humbleness and entire devotion I pray to Thee to make me a minaret of Thy love in Thy land, a lamp of Thy knowledge among Thy creatures, and a banner of divine bounty in Thy dominion.

Number me with such of Thy servants as have detached themselves from everything but Thee, have sanctified themselves from the transitory things of this world, and have freed themselves from the promptings of the voicers of idle fancies.

Let my heart be dilated with joy through the spirit of confirmation from Thy kingdom, and brighten my eyes by beholding the hosts of divine assistance descending successively upon me from the kingdom of Thine omnipotent glory. Thou art, in truth, the Almighty, the All-Glorious, the All-Powerful

—'Abdu'l-Bahá

"Rely upon God. Trust in Him. Praise Him, and call Him continually to mind. He verily turneth trouble into ease, and sorrow into solace, and toil into utter peace. He verily hath dominion over all things."

—'Abdu'l-Bahá

THE DEPARTED

OBLIGATORY PRAYER FOR THE DEAD

The obligatory Prayer for the Dead is to be used for Bahá'ís over the age of fifteen. "It is the only Bahá'í obligatory prayer which is to be recited in congregation; it is to be recited by one believer while all present stand in silence...that the recital should precede the interment.., that there is no requirement to face the Qiblih..."

—Bahá'u'lláh, Kitáb-i-Aqdas

O my God! *This is Thy servant and the son of Thy servant* [1] who hath believed in Thee and in Thy signs, and set his face towards Thee, wholly detached from all except Thee. Thou art, verily, of those who show mercy the most merciful.

Deal with him, O Thou Who forgivest the sins of men and concealest their faults, as beseemeth the heaven of Thy bounty and the ocean of Thy grace. Grant him admission within the precincts of Thy transcendent mercy that was before the

---

1 If the dead be a woman, let him say: *This is Thy handmaiden and the daughter of Thy handmaiden, etc...*

foundation of earth and heaven. There is no God but Thee, the Ever-Forgiving, the Most Generous.

Let him, then, repeat six times the greeting "Alláh-u-Abhá" and then repeat nineteen times each of the following verses: * (read note below)

We all, verily, worship God.

We all, verily, bow down before God.

We all, verily, are devoted unto God.

We all, verily, give praise unto God.

We all, verily, yield thanks unto God.

We all, verily, are patient in God.

—Bahá'u'lláh

* In other words, the six repetitions of "Alláh-u-Abhá" proceed as follows:

"Alláh-u-Abhá" (once),

"We all, verily, Worship God" (19 times),

"Alláh-u-Abhá" (once).

"We all, verily, bow down before God" (19 times), and so on.

GENERAL PRAYERS FOR THE DEPARTED

Glory be to Thee, O Lord my God! Abase not him whom Thou hast exalted through the power of Thine everlasting sovereignty, and remove not far from Thee him whom Thou hast caused to enter the tabernacle of Thine eternity. Wilt Thou cast away, O my God, him whom Thou hast overshadowed with Thy Lordship, and wilt Thou turn away from Thee, O my Desire, him to whom Thou hast been a refuge? Canst Thou degrade him whom Thou hast uplifted, or forget him whom Thou didst enable to remember Thee?

Glorified, immensely glorified art Thou! Thou art He Who from everlasting hath been the King of the entire creation and its Prime Mover, and Thou wilt to everlasting remain the Lord of all created things and their Ordainer. Glorified art Thou, O my God! If Thou ceasest to be merciful unto Thy servants, who, then, will show mercy unto them; and if Thou refusest to succor Thy loved ones, who is there that can succor them?

Glorified, immeasurably glorified art Thou! Thou art adored in Thy truth, and Thee do we all, verily, worship; and Thou art manifest in Thy justice, and to Thee do we all, verily, bear witness. Thou art, in truth, beloved in Thy grace. No God is there but Thee, the Help in Peril, the Self-Subsisting. —Bahá'u'lláh

O my God! O Thou forgiver of sins, bestower of gifts, dispeller of afflictions! Verily, I beseech Thee to forgive the sins of such as have abandoned the physical garment and have ascended to the spiritual world.

O my Lord! Purify them from trespasses, dispel their sorrows, and change their darkness into light. Cause them to enter the garden of happiness, cleanse them with the most pure water, and grant them to behold Thy splendors on the loftiest mount. —'Abdu'l-Bahá

"Know thou of a truth that the soul, after its separation from the body, will continue to progress until it attaineth the presence of God... It will endure as long as the Kingdom of God, His sovereignty, His dominion and power will endure." —Bahá'u'lláh

FOR WOMEN

O Lord, O Thou Whose mercy hath encompassed all, Whose forgiveness is transcendent, Whose bounty is sublime, Whose pardon and generosity are all-embracing, and the lights of Whose forgiveness are diffused throughout the world! O Lord of Glory! I entreat Thee, fervently and tearfully, to cast upon Thy handmaiden who hath ascended unto Thee the glances of the eye of Thy mercy. Robe her in the mantle of Thy grace, bright with the ornaments of the celestial Paradise, and, sheltering her beneath the tree of Thy oneness, illumine her face with the lights of Thy mercy and compassion.

Bestow upon Thy heavenly handmaiden, O God, the holy fragrances born of the spirit of Thy forgiveness. Cause her to dwell in a blissful abode, heal her griefs with the balm of Thy reunion, and, in accordance with Thy will, grant her admission to Thy holy Paradise. Let the angels of Thy loving-kindness descend successively upon her, and shelter her beneath Thy blessed Tree. Thou art, verily, the Ever-Forgiving, the Most Generous, the All-Bountiful.

—'Abdu'l-Bahá

O my God, O Forgiver of sins and Dispeller of afflictions! O Thou Who art the Pardoner, the Merciful! I raise my suppliant hands to Thee, tearfully beseeching the court of Thy divine Essence to forgive, through Thy grace and clemency, Thy handmaiden who hath ascended unto the seat of truth. Cause her, O Lord, to be overshadowed by the clouds of Thy bounty and favor, immerse her in the ocean of Thy forgiveness and pardon, and enable her to enter that sanctified abode, Thy heavenly Paradise.

Thou art, verily, the Mighty, the Compassionate, the Generous, the Merciful. —'Abdu'l-Bahá

"*Death proffereth unto every confident believer the cup that is life indeed. It bestoweth joy, and is the bearer of gladness. It conferreth the gift of everlasting life.*" —Bahá'u'lláh

FIRMNESS IN THE COVENANT

"O ye beloved of God, know that steadfastness and firmness in this new and wonderful Covenant is indeed the spirit that quickeneth the hearts which are overflowing with the love of the Glorious Lord; verily, it is the power which penetrates into the hearts of the people of the world!" —'Abdu'l-Bahá

We pray to God to graciously assist them that have been led astray to be just and fair-minded, and to make them aware of that whereof they have been heedless. He, in truth, is the All-Bounteous, the Most Generous. Debar not Thy servants, O my Lord, from the door of Thy grace, and drive them not away from the court of Thy presence. Assist them to dispel the mists of idle fancy, and to tear away the veils of vain imaginings and hopes. Thou art, verily, the All-Possessing, the Most High. No God is there but Thee, the Almighty, the Gracious.

—Bahá'u'lláh

Make firm our steps, O Lord, in Thy path and strengthen Thou our hearts in Thine obedience. Turn our faces toward the beauty of Thy oneness, and gladden our bosoms with the signs of Thy divine unity. Adorn our bodies with the robe of Thy bounty, and remove from our eyes the veil of sinfulness, and give us the chalice of Thy grace; that the essence of all beings may sing Thy praise before the vision of Thy grandeur. Reveal then Thyself, O Lord, by Thy merciful utterance and the mystery of Thy divine being, that the holy ecstasy of prayer may fill our souls - a prayer that shall rise above words and letters and transcend the murmur of syllables and sounds - that all things may be merged into nothingness before the revelation of Thy splendor.

Lord! These are servants that have remained fast and firm in Thy Covenant and Thy Testament, that have held fast unto the cord of constancy in Thy Cause and clung unto the hem of the robe of Thy grandeur. Assist them, O Lord, with Thy grace, confirm with Thy power and strengthen their loins in obedience to Thee. Thou art the Pardoner, the Gracious.

—'Abdu'l-Bahá

O Thou beloved of my heart and soul! I have no refuge save thee. I raise no voice at dawn except in Thy commemoration and praise. Thy love encompasseth me and Thy Grace is perfect. My hope is in Thee. O God, give me a new life at every instant and bestow upon me the breaths of the Holy Spirit at every moment, in order that I may remain steadfast in Thy love; attain unto great felicity, perceive the manifest light and be in the state of utmost tranquility and submissiveness. Verily, Thou art the Giver, the Forgiver, the Compassionate. —'Abdu'l-Bahá

O my Lord and my Hope! Help Thou Thy loved ones to be steadfast in Thy mighty Covenant, to remain faithful to Thy manifest Cause, and to carry out the commandments Thou didst set down for them in Thy Book of Splendors; that they may become banners of guidance and lamps of the Company above, wellsprings of Thine infinite wisdom, and stars that lead aright, as they shine down from the supernal sky. Verily, Thou art the Invincible the Almighty, the All-Powerful.

—'Abdu'l-Bahá

FORGIVENESS

"All forgiveness floweth, in this Day, from God, Him to Whom none can compare, with Whom no partners can be joined, the Sovereign Protector of all men, and the Concealer of their sins!" —Bahá'u'lláh

When the sinner findeth himself wholly detached and freed from all save God, he should beg forgiveness and pardon from Him... Verily He is the Compassionate, the Merciful. The sinner should, between himself and God, implore mercy from the Ocean of mercy, beg forgiveness from the Heaven of generosity and say:

O God, my God! I implore Thee by the blood of Thy true lovers who were so enraptured by Thy sweet utterance that they hastened unto the Pinnacle of Glory, the site of the most glorious martyrdom, and I beseech Thee by the mysteries which lie enshrined in Thy knowledge and by the pearls that are treasured in the ocean of Thy bounty to grant forgiveness unto me and unto my father and my mother. Of those who show forth mercy, Thou art in truth the Most Merciful. No God is there but Thee, the Ever-Forgiving, the All-Bountiful.

O Lord! Thou seest this essence of sinfulness turning unto the ocean of Thy favor and this feeble one seeking the kingdom of Thy divine power and this poor creature inclining himself towards the day-star of Thy wealth. By Thy mercy and Thy grace, disappoint him not, O Lord, nor debar him from the revelations of Thy bounty in Thy days, nor cast him away from Thy door which Thou hast opened wide to all that dwell in Thy heaven and on Thine earth. Alas! Alas! My sins have prevented me from approaching the Court of Thy holiness and my trespasses have caused me to stray far from the Tabernacle of Thy majesty. I have committed that which Thou didst forbid me to do and have put away what Thou didst order me to observe. I pray Thee by Him Who is the sovereign Lord of Names to write down for me with the Pen of Thy bounty that which will enable me to draw nigh unto Thee and will purge me from my trespasses which have intervened between me and Thy forgiveness and Thy pardon. Verily, Thou art the Potent, the Bountiful. No God is there but Thee, the Mighty, the Gracious.

—Bahá'u'lláh

Praise be unto Thee, O Lord. Forgive us our sins, have mercy upon us and enable us to return unto Thee. Suffer us not to rely on aught else besides Thee, and vouchsafe unto us, through Thy bounty, that which Thou lovest and desirest and well beseemeth Thee. Exalt the station of them that have truly believed and forgive them with Thy gracious forgiveness. Verily Thou art the Help in Peril, the Self-Subsisting. —The Báb

O my God, O my Lord, O my Master! I beg Thee to forgive me for seeking any pleasure save Thy love, or any comfort except Thy nearness, or any delight besides Thy good-pleasure, or any existence other than communion with Thee.

—The Báb

O Thou forgiving Lord! Thou art the shelter of all these Thy servants. Thou knowest the secrets and art aware of all things. We are all helpless, and Thou art the Mighty, the Omnipotent. We are all sinners, and Thou art the Forgiver of sins, the Merciful, the Compassionate. O Lord! Look not at our shortcomings. Deal with us according to Thy grace and bounty. Our shortcomings are many, but the ocean of Thy forgiveness is boundless. Our weakness is grievous, but the evidences of Thine aid and assistance are clear. Therefore, confirm and strengthen us. Enable us to do that which is worthy of Thy holy Threshold. Illumine our hearts, grant us discerning eyes and attentive ears. Resuscitate the dead and heal the sick. Bestow wealth upon the poor and give peace and security to the fearful. Accept us in Thy kingdom and illumine us with the light of guidance. Thou art the Powerful and the Omnipotent. Thou art the Generous. Thou art the Clement. Thou art the Kind.

—'Abdu'l-Bahá

"*Confession of sins and transgressions before human beings is not permissible, as it hath never been nor will ever be conducive to divine forgiveness. Moreover such confession before people results in one's humiliation and abasement, and God—exalted be His glory—wisheth not the humiliation of His servants.*"

—Bahá'u'lláh

THE FUND

"All the friends of God... should contribute to the extent possible, however modest their offering may be. God doth not burden a soul beyond its capacity. O Friends of God! Be ye assured that in place of these contributions, your agriculture, your industry, and your commerce will be blessed by manifold increases, with goodly gifts and bestowals. He who cometh with one goodly deed will receive a tenfold reward."

—'Abdu'l-Bahá

O God, my God! Illumine the brows of Thy true lovers, and support them with angelic hosts of certain triumph. Set firm their feet on Thy straight path, and out of Thine ancient bounty open before them the portals of Thy blessings; for they are expending on Thy pathway what Thou hast bestowed upon them, safeguarding Thy Faith, putting their trust in their remembrance of Thee, offering up their hearts for love of Thee, and withholding not what they possess in adoration for Thy Beauty and in their search for ways to please Thee. O my Lord! Ordain for them a plenteous share, a destined recompense and sure reward. Verily, Thou art the Sustainer, the Helper, the Generous, the Bountiful, the Ever-Bestowing. —'Abdu'l-Bahá

ḤUQÚQU'LLÁH

THE RIGHT OF GOD

"Ḥuqúqu'lláh is indeed a great law. It is incumbent upon all to make this offering, because it is the source of grace, abundance, and of all good. It is a bounty which shall remain with every soul in every world of the worlds of God, the All-Possessing, the All-Bountiful."

—Bahá'u'lláh

Magnified art Thou, O Lord of the entire creation, the One unto Whom all things must turn. With my inner and outer tongues I bear witness that Thou hast manifested and revealed Thyself, sent down Thy signs, and proclaimed Thy testimonies. I testify to Thy self-sufficiency from aught else except Thee, and Thy sanctity above all earthly things. I entreat Thee by the transcendent glory of Thy Cause and the supreme potency of Thy Word to grant confirmation unto him who desireth to offer what Thou hast prescribed unto him in Thy Book and to observe that which will shed forth the fragrance of Thine acceptance. Verily Thou art the All-Mighty, the All-Gracious, the All-Forgiving, the All-Generous. —Bahá'u'lláh

HANDS OF THE CAUSE OF GOD

"...the Chief Stewards of Bahá'u'lláh's embryonic World Commonwealth, who have been invested by the unerring Pen of the Centre of His Covenant with the dual function of guarding over the security, and of insuring the propagation, of His Father's Faith."

—Shoghi Effendi

Light and glory, greeting and praise be upon the Hands of His Cause, through whom the light of fortitude hath shone forth and the truth hath been established that the authority to choose rests with God, the Powerful, the Mighty, the Unconstrained, through whom the ocean of bounty hath surged and the fragrance of the gracious favors of God, the Lord of mankind, hath been diffused. We beseech Him – exalted is He – to shield them through the power of His hosts, to protect them through the potency of His dominion and to aid them through His indomitable strength which prevaileth over all created things. Sovereignty is God's, the Creator of the heavens and the Lord of the Kingdom of Names. —Bahá'u'lláh

HAPPINESS & TRANQUILITY

Create in me a pure heart, O my God, and renew a tranquil conscience within me, O my Hope! Through the spirit of power confirm Thou me in Thy Cause, O my Best-Beloved, and by the light of Thy glory reveal unto me Thy path, O Thou the Goal of my desire! Through the power of Thy transcendent might lift me up unto the heaven of Thy holiness, O Source of my being, and by the breezes of Thine eternity gladden me, O Thou Who art my God! Let Thine everlasting melodies breathe tranquility on me, O my Companion, and let the riches of Thine ancient countenance deliver me from all except Thee, O my Master, and let the tidings of the revelation of Thine incorruptible Essence bring me joy, O Thou Who art the most manifest of the manifest and the most hidden of the hidden!

—Bahá'u'lláh

Make me ready, in all circumstances, O my Lord, to serve Thee and to set myself towards the adored sanctuary of Thy Revelation and of Thy Beauty. If it be Thy pleasure, make me to grow as a tender herb in the meadows of Thy grace, that the gentle winds of Thy will may stir me up and bend me into conformity with Thy pleasure, in such wise that my movement and my stillness may be wholly directed by Thee.

—Bahá'u'lláh

O God! Refresh and gladden my spirit. Purify my heart. Illumine my powers. I lay all my affairs in Thy hand. Thou art my Guide and my Refuge. I will no longer be sorrowful and grieved; I will be a happy and joyful being. O God! I will no longer be full of anxiety, nor will I let trouble harass me. I will not dwell on the unpleasant things of life.

O God! Thou art more friend to me than I am to myself. I dedicate myself to Thee, O Lord.

—Attributed to 'Abdu'l-Bahá

"Joy gives us wings! In times of joy our strength is more vital, our intellect keener, and our understanding less clouded."

—'Abdu'l-Bahá

HEALING

"The prayers which were revealed to ask for healing apply both the physical and spiritual healing. Recite them, then, to heal both the soul and the body."

—'Abdu'l-Bahá

Thy name is my healing, O my God, and remembrance of Thee is my remedy. Nearness to Thee is my hope, and love for Thee is my companion. Thy mercy to me is my healing and my succor in both this world and the world to come. Thou, verily, art the All-Bountiful, the All-Knowing, the All-Wise. —Bahá'u'lláh

FOR INFANTS

Thou art He, O my God, through Whose names the sick are healed and the ailing are restored, and the thirsty are given drink, and the sore-vexed are tranquillized, and the wayward are guided, and the abased are exalted, and the poor are enriched, and the ignorant are enlightened, and the gloomy are illumined, and the sorrowful are cheered, and the chilled are warmed, and the downtrodden are raised up. Through Thy name, O my God, all created things were stirred up, and the heavens were spread, and the earth was established, and the clouds were raised and made to rain upon the earth. This, verily, is a token of Thy grace unto all Thy creatures.

I implore Thee, therefore, by Thy name through which Thou didst manifest Thy Godhead, and didst exalt Thy Cause above all creation, and by each of Thy most excellent titles and most august attributes, and by all the virtues wherewith Thy transcendent and most exalted Being is extolled, to send down this night from the clouds of Thy mercy the rains of Thy healing upon this suckling, whom Thou hast related unto Thine all-glorious Self in the kingdom of Thy creation.

Clothe him, then, O my God, by Thy grace, with the robe of well-being and health, and guard him, O my Beloved, from every affliction and disorder, and from whatever is obnoxious unto Thee. Thy might, verily, is equal to all things. Thou, in truth, art the Most Powerful, the Self-Subsisting.

Send down, moreover, upon him, O my God, the good of this world and of the next, and the good of the former and latter generations. Thy might and Thy wisdom are, verily, equal unto this.

—Bahá'u'lláh

FOR WOMEN

Glory be to Thee, O Lord my God! I beg of Thee by Thy Name through which He Who is Thy Beauty hath been stablished upon the throne of Thy Cause, and by Thy Name through which Thou changest all things, and gatherest together all things, and callest to account all things, and rewardest all things, and preservest all things, and sustainest all things—I beg of Thee to guard this handmaiden who hath fled for refuge to Thee, and hath sought the shelter of Him in Whom Thou Thyself art manifest, and hath put her whole trust and confidence in Thee.

She is sick, O my God, and hath entered beneath the shadow of the Tree of Thy healing; afflicted, and hath fled to the City of Thy protection; diseased, and hath sought the Fountainhead of Thy favors; sorely vexed, and hath hasted to attain the Wellspring of Thy tranquility; burdened with sin, and hath set her face toward the court of Thy forgiveness.

Attire her, by Thy sovereignty and Thy loving-kindness, O my God and my Beloved, with the raiment of Thy balm and Thy healing, and make her quaff of the cup of Thy mercy and Thy favors. Protect her, moreover, from every affliction and ailment, from all pain and sickness, and from whatsoever may be abhorrent unto Thee.

Thou, in truth, art immensely exalted above all else except Thyself. Thou art, verily, the Healer, the All-Sufficing, the Preserver, the Ever-Forgiving, the Most Merciful. —Bahá'u'lláh

"There are two ways of healing sickness, material means and spiritual means. The first is by the treatment of physicians; the second consisteth in prayers offered by the spiritual ones to God and in turning to Him. Both means should be used and practiced."

"If thou art desirous of health, wish thou health for serving the Kingdom ... that thou mayest drink from the fountain of eternal life and be assisted by the spirit of divine confirmation..." —'Abdu'l-Bahá

THE LONG HEALING PRAYER

He is the Healer, the Sufficer, the Helper,
the All-Forgiving, the All-Merciful.

I call on Thee O Exalted One,
O Faithful One, O Glorious One!
Thou the Sufficing, Thou the Healing,
Thou the Abiding, O Thou Abiding One!

I call on Thee O Sovereign, O Upraiser, O Judge!
Thou the Sufficing, Thou the Healing,
Thou the Abiding, O Thou Abiding One!

I call on Thee O Peerless One,
O Eternal One, O Single One!
Thou the Sufficing, Thou the Healing,
Thou the Abiding, O Thou Abiding One!

I call on Thee O Most Praised One,
O Holy One, O Helping One!
Thou the Sufficing, Thou the Healing,
Thou the Abiding, O Thou Abiding One!

I call on Thee O Omniscient,
O Most Wise, O Most Great One!
Thou the Sufficing, Thou the Healing,
Thou the Abiding, O Thou Abiding One!

I call on Thee O Clement One,
O Majestic One, O Ordaining One!
Thou the Sufficing, Thou the Healing,
Thou the Abiding, O Thou Abiding One!

I call on Thee O Beloved One,
O Cherished One, O Enraptured One!
Thou the Sufficing, Thou the Healing,
Thou the Abiding, O Thou Abiding One!

I call on Thee O Mightiest One,
O Sustaining One, O Potent One!
Thou the Sufficing, Thou the Healing,
Thou the Abiding, O Thou Abiding One!

I call on Thee O Ruling One,
O Self-Subsisting, O All-Knowing One!
Thou the Sufficing, Thou the Healing,
Thou the Abiding, O Thou Abiding One!

I call on Thee O Spirit, O Light,
O Most Manifest One!
Thou the Sufficing, Thou the Healing,
Thou the Abiding, O Thou Abiding One!

I call on Thee O Thou Frequented by all,
O Thou Known to all, O Thou Hidden from all!

Thou the Sufficing, Thou the Healing,
Thou the Abiding, O Thou Abiding One!

I call on Thee O Concealed One,
O Triumphant One, O Bestowing One!
Thou the Sufficing, Thou the Healing,
Thou the Abiding, O Thou Abiding One!

I call on Thee O Almighty,
O Succoring One, O Concealing One!
Thou the Sufficing, Thou the Healing,
Thou the Abiding, O Thou Abiding One!

I call on Thee O Fashioner,
O Satisfier, O Uprooter!
Thou the Sufficing, Thou the Healing,
Thou the Abiding, O Thou Abiding One!

I call on Thee O Rising One,
O Gathering One, O Exalting One!
Thou the Sufficing, Thou the Healing,
Thou the Abiding, O Thou Abiding One!

I call on Thee O Perfecting One,
O Unfettered One, O Bountiful One!
Thou the Sufficing, Thou the Healing,
Thou the Abiding, O Thou Abiding One!

I call on Thee O Beneficent One,
O Withholding One, O Creating One!
Thou the Sufficing, Thou the Healing,
Thou the Abiding, O Thou Abiding One!

I call on Thee O Most Sublime One,
O Beauteous One, O Bounteous One!
Thou the Sufficing, Thou the Healing,
Thou the Abiding, O Thou Abiding One!

I call on Thee O Just One,
O Gracious One, O Generous One!
Thou the Sufficing, Thou the Healing,
Thou the Abiding, O Thou Abiding One!

I call on Thee O All-Compelling,
O Ever-Abiding, O Most Knowing One!
Thou the Sufficing, Thou the Healing,
Thou the Abiding, O Thou Abiding One!

I call on Thee O Magnificent One,
O Ancient of Days, O Magnanimous One!
Thou the Sufficing, Thou the Healing,
Thou the Abiding, O Thou Abiding One!

I call on Thee O Well-guarded One,
O Lord of Joy, O Desired One!

Thou the Sufficing, Thou the Healing,
Thou the Abiding, O Thou Abiding One!

I call on Thee O Thou Kind to all,
O Thou Compassionate with all,
O Most Benevolent One!
Thou the Sufficing, Thou the Healing,
Thou the Abiding, O Thou Abiding One!

I call on Thee O Haven for all,
O Shelter to all, O All-Preserving One!
Thou the Sufficing, Thou the Healing,
Thou the Abiding, O Thou Abiding One!

I call on Thee O Thou Succorer of all,
O Thou Invoked by all, O Quickening One!
Thou the Sufficing, Thou the Healing,
Thou the Abiding, O Thou Abiding One!

I call on Thee O Unfolder, O Ravager,
O Most Clement One!
Thou the Sufficing, Thou the Healing,
Thou the Abiding, O Thou Abiding One!

I call on Thee O Thou my Soul,
O Thou my Beloved, O Thou my Faith!
Thou the Sufficing, Thou the Healing,

Thou the Abiding, O Thou Abiding One!

I call on Thee O Quencher of thirsts,
O Transcendent Lord, O Most Precious One!
Thou the Sufficing, Thou the Healing,
Thou the Abiding, O Thou Abiding One!

I call on Thee O Greatest Remembrance,
O Noblest Name, O Most Ancient Way!
Thou the Sufficing, Thou the Healing,
Thou the Abiding, O Thou Abiding One!

I call on Thee O Most Lauded,
O Most Holy, O Sanctified One!
Thou the Sufficing, Thou the Healing,
Thou the Abiding, O Thou Abiding One!

I call on Thee O Unfastener,
O Counselor, O Deliverer!
Thou the Sufficing, Thou the Healing,
Thou the Abiding, O Thou Abiding One!

I call on Thee O Friend, O Physician,
O Captivating One!
Thou the Sufficing, Thou the Healing,
Thou the Abiding, O Thou Abiding One!

I call on Thee O Glory, O Beauty,

O Bountiful One!
Thou the Sufficing, Thou the Healing,
Thou the Abiding, O Thou Abiding One!

I call on Thee O the Most Trusted,
O the Best Lover, O Lord of the Dawn!
Thou the Sufficing, Thou the Healing,
Thou the Abiding, O Thou Abiding One!

I call on Thee O Enkindler,
O Brightener, O Bringer of Delight!
Thou the Sufficing, Thou the Healing,
Thou the Abiding, O Thou Abiding One!

I call on Thee O Lord of Bounty,
O Most Compassionate, O Most Merciful One!
Thou the Sufficing, Thou the Healing,
Thou the Abiding, O Thou Abiding One!

I call on Thee O Constant One,
O Life-Giving One, O Source of all Being!
Thou the Sufficing, Thou the Healing,
Thou the Abiding, O Thou Abiding One!

I call on Thee O Thou Who penetratest all things,
O All-Seeing God, O Lord of Utterance!
Thou the Sufficing, Thou the Healing,
Thou the Abiding, O Thou Abiding One!

I call on Thee O Manifest yet Hidden,
O Unseen yet Renowned, O Onlooker sought by all! Thou the Sufficing, Thou the Healing,
Thou the Abiding, O Thou Abiding One!

I call on Thee O Thou Who slayest the Lovers,
O God of Grace to the wicked!

O Sufficer, I call on Thee, O Sufficer!
O Healer, I call on Thee, O Healer!
O Abider, I call on Thee, O Abider!
Thou the Ever-Abiding, O Thou Abiding One!

Sanctified art Thou, O my God! I beseech Thee by Thy generosity, whereby the portals of Thy bounty and grace were opened wide, whereby the Temple of Thy Holiness was established upon the throne of eternity; and by Thy mercy whereby Thou didst invite all created things unto the table of Thy bounties and bestowals; and by Thy grace whereby Thou didst respond, in thine own Self with Thy word "Yea!" on behalf of all in heaven and earth, at the hour when Thy sovereignty and Thy grandeur stood revealed, at the dawn-time when the might of Thy dominion was made manifest.

And again do I beseech Thee, by these most beauteous names, by these most noble and sublime attributes, and by Thy most Exalted Remembrance, and by Thy pure and spotless Beauty, and by Thy hidden Light in the most hidden pavilion, and by Thy Name, cloaked with the garment of affliction every morn and eve, to protect the bearer of this blessed Tablet, and whoso reciteth it, and whoso cometh upon it, and whoso passeth around the house wherein it is.

Heal Thou, then, by it every sick, diseased and poor one, from every tribulation and distress, from every loathsome affliction and sorrow, and guide Thou by it whosoever desireth to enter upon the paths of Thy guidance, and the ways of Thy forgiveness and grace.

Thou art verily the Powerful, the All-Sufficing, the Healing, the Protector, the Giving, the Compassionate, the All-Generous, the All-Merciful.

—Bahá'u'lláh

HUMANITY

O Thou kind Lord! Thou hast created all humanity from the same stock. Thou hast decreed that all shall belong to the same household. In Thy Holy Presence they are all Thy servants, and all mankind are sheltered beneath Thy Tabernacle; all have gathered together at Thy Table of Bounty; all are illumined through the light of Thy Providence.

O God! Thou art kind to all, Thou hast provided for all, dost shelter all, conferrest life upon all. Thou hast endowed each and all with talents and faculties, and all are submerged in the Ocean of Thy Mercy.

O Thou kind Lord! Unite all. Let the religions agree and make the nations one, so that they may see each other as one family and the whole earth as one home. May they all live together in perfect harmony.

O God! Raise aloft the banner of the oneness of mankind. O God! Establish the Most Great Peace. Cement Thou, O God, the hearts together.

O Thou kind Father, God! Gladden our hearts through the fragrance of Thy love. Brighten our eyes through the Light of Thy Guidance. Delight our ears with the melody of Thy Word, and shelter us all in the Stronghold of Thy Providence.

Thou art the Mighty and Powerful, Thou art the Forgiving and Thou art the One Who overlooketh the shortcomings of all mankind. —'Abdu'l-Bahá

O God! we are weak; give us strength. We are poor; bestow upon us Thine illimitable treasures. We are sick; grant us Thy divine healing. We are powerless; give us of Thy heavenly power. O Lord! Make us useful in this world; free us from the condition of self and desire.

O Lord! Make us firm in Thy love and cause us to be loving toward the whole of mankind. Confirm us in service to the world of humanity, so that we may become the servants of Thy servants, that we may love all Thy creatures and become compassionate to all Thy people. O Lord! Thou art the Almighty! Thou art the Merciful! Thou art the Forgiver! Thou art the Omnipotent. —'Abdu'l-Bahá

HUSBANDS

O God, my God! This Thy handmaid is calling upon Thee, trusting in Thee, turning her face unto Thee, imploring Thee to shed Thy heavenly bounties upon her, and to disclose unto her Thy spiritual mysteries, and to cast upon her the lights of Thy Godhead.

O my Lord! Make the eyes of my husband to see. Rejoice Thou his heart with the light of the knowledge of Thee, draw Thou his mind unto Thy luminous beauty, cheer Thou his spirit by revealing unto him Thy manifest splendors.

O my Lord! Lift Thou the veil from before his sight. Rain down Thy plenteous bounties upon him, intoxicate him with the wine of love for Thee, make him one of Thy angels whose feet walk upon this earth even as their souls are soaring through the high heavens. Cause him to become a brilliant lamp, shining out with the light of Thy wisdom in the midst of Thy people.

Verily Thou art the Precious, the Ever-Bestowing, the Open of Hand. —'Abdu'l-Bahá

JOURNEY

I have risen this morning by Thy grace, O my God, and left my home trusting wholly in Thee, and committing myself to Thy care. Send down, then, upon me, out of the heaven of Thy mercy, a blessing from Thy side, and enable me to return home in safety even as Thou didst enable me to set out under Thy protection with my thoughts fixed steadfastly upon Thee. There is none other God but Thee, the One, the Incomparable, the All-Knowing, the All-Wise.

—Bahá'u'lláh

O God, my God! I have set out from my home, holding fast unto the cord of Thy love, and I have committed myself wholly to Thy care and Thy protection. I entreat Thee by Thy power through which Thou didst protect Thy loved ones from the wayward and the perverse, and from every contumacious oppressor, and every wicked doer who hath strayed far from Thee, to keep me safe by Thy bounty and thy grace. Enable me, then, to return to my home by Thy power and Thy might. Thou art, truly, the Almighty, the Help in Peril, the Self-Subsisting.

—Bahá'u'lláh

KNOWLEDGE

O God, O Thou Who hast cast Thy splendor over the luminous realities of men, shedding upon them the resplendent lights of knowledge and guidance, and hast chosen them out of all created things for this supernal grace, and hast caused them to encompass all things, to understand their inmost essence, and to disclose their mysteries, bringing them forth out of darkness into the visible world! "He verily showeth His special mercy to whomsoever He will."[1] O Lord, help Thou Thy loved ones to acquire knowledge and the sciences and arts, and to unravel the secrets that are treasured up in the inmost reality of all created beings. Make them to hear the hidden truths that are written and embedded in the heart of all that is. Make them to be ensigns of guidance amongst all creatures and piercing rays of the mind shedding forth their light in this, the "first life."[2] Make them to be leaders unto Thee, guides unto Thy path, runners urging men on to Thy Kingdom.

Thou verily art the Powerful, the Protector, the Potent, the Defender, the Mighty, the Most Generous.

—'Abdu'l-Bahá

---

1 Qur'án 51:56

2 Qur'án 55:19-22

MARRIAGE

"Bahá'í marriage is union and cordial affection between the two parties. They must, however, exercise the utmost care and become acquainted with each other's character. This eternal bond should be made secure by a firm covenant, and the intention should be to foster harmony, fellowship and unity and to attain everlasting life." —'Abdu'l-Bahá

The pledge of marriage, the verse to be spoken individually by the bride and the bridegroom in the presence of at least two witnesses acceptable to the Spiritual Assembly is, as stipulated in the Kitáb-i-Aqdas [The Most Holy Book]:

"We will all, verily, abide by the Will of God."

He is the Bestower, the Bounteous! Praise be to God, the Ancient, the Ever-Abiding, the Changeless, the Eternal! He Who hath testified in His Own Being that verily He is the One, the Single, the Untrammeled, the Exalted. We bear witness that verily there is no God but Him, acknowledging His oneness, confessing His singleness. He hath ever dwelt in unapproachable heights, in the summits of His loftiness, sanctified from the mention of aught save Himself, free from the description of aught but Him.

And when He desired to manifest grace and beneficence to men, and to set the world in order, He revealed observances and created laws; among them He established the law of marriage, made it as a fortress for well-being and salvation, and enjoined it upon us in that which was sent down out of the heaven of sanctity in His Most Holy Book. He saith, great is His glory:

"Enter into wedlock, O people, that ye may bring forth one who will make mention of Me amid My servants. This is My bidding unto you; hold fast to it as an assistance to yourselves."

—Bahá'u'lláh

Glory be unto Thee, O my God! Verily, this Thy servant and this Thy maidservant have gathered under the shadow of Thy mercy and they are united through Thy favor and generosity.

O Lord! Assist them in this Thy world and Thy kingdom and destine for them every good through Thy bounty and grace.

O Lord! Confirm them in Thy servitude and assist them in Thy service. Suffer them to become the signs of Thy Name in Thy world and protect them through Thy bestowals which are inexhaustible in this world and the world to come.

O Lord! They are supplicating the kingdom of Thy mercifulness and invoking the realm of Thy singleness.

Verily, they are married in obedience to Thy command. Cause them to become the signs of harmony and unity until the end of time. Verily, Thou art the Omnipotent, the Omnipresent and the Almighty!

—'Abdu'l-Bahá

He is God! O peerless Lord! In Thine almighty wisdom Thou hast enjoined marriage upon the peoples, that the generations of men may succeed one another in this contingent world, and that ever, so long as the world shall last, they may busy themselves at the Threshold of Thy oneness with servitude and worship, with salutation, adoration and praise. "I have not created spirits and men, but that they should worship me." Wherefore, wed Thou in the heaven of Thy mercy these two birds of the nest of Thy love, and make them the means of attracting perpetual grace; that from the union of these two seas of love a wave of tenderness may surge and cast the pearls of pure and goodly issue on the shore of life. "He hath let loose the two seas, that they meet each other: Between them is a barrier which they overpass not. Which then of the bounties of your Lord will ye deny? From each He bringeth up greater and lesser pearls."

O Thou kind Lord! Make Thou this marriage to bring forth coral and pearls. Thou art verily the All-Powerful, the Most Great, the Ever-Forgiving.

—'Abdu'l-Bahá

MARTYRS & THEIR FAMILIES

He is God! O Lord my God! O Thou Helper of the feeble, Succorer of the poor and Deliverer of the helpless who turn unto Thee.

With utmost lowliness I raise my suppliant hands to Thy kingdom of beauty and fervently call upon Thee with my inner tongue, saying:

O God, my God! Aid me to adore Thee; strengthen my loins to serve Thee; assist me by Thy grace in my servitude to Thee; suffer me to remain steadfast in my obedience to Thee; pour forth upon me the liberal effusions of Thy bounty, let the glances of the eye of Thy loving-kindness be directed towards me, and immerse me in the ocean of Thy forgiveness. Grant that I may be confirmed in my allegiance to Thy Faith, and bestow upon me a fuller measure of certitude and assurance, that I may wholly dispense with the world, may turn my face with entire devotion towards Thy face, be reinforced by the compelling power of proofs and testimonies, and, invested with majesty and power, may pass beyond every region of heaven and earth. Verily Thou art the Merciful, the All-

Glorious, the Kind, the Compassionate.

O Lord! These are the survivors of the martyrs, that company of blessed souls. They have sustained every tribulation and displayed patience in the face of grievous injustice. They have forsaken all comfort and prosperity, have willingly submitted to dire suffering and adversity in the path of Thy love, and are still held captive in the clutches of their enemies who continually torment them with sore torment, and oppress them because they walk steadfastly in Thy straight path. There is no one to help them, no one to befriend them. Apart from the ignoble and the wicked, there is no one to associate and consort with them.

O Lord! These souls have tasted bitter agony in this earthly life and have, as a sign of their love for the shining beauty of Thy countenance and in their eagerness to attain Thy celestial kingdom, tolerated every gross indignity that the people of tyranny have inflicted upon them.

O Lord! Fill their ears with the verses of divine assistance and of a speedy victory, and deliver them from the oppression of such as wield terrible might. Withhold the hands of the wicked, and leave not these souls to be torn by the claws and teeth of fierce beasts, for they are captivated by their love for Thee, entrusted with the mysteries of Thy holiness, stand humbly at Thy door and have attained to Thine exalted precinct.

O Lord! Graciously reinforce them with a new spirit; illumine their eyes by enabling them to behold Thy wondrous evidences in the gloom of night; destine for them all good that aboundeth in Thy Kingdom of eternal mysteries; make them as brilliant stars shining over all regions, luxuriant trees laden with fruit and branches moving in the breezes of dawn. Verily, Thou art the Bountiful, the Mighty, the Omnipotent, the Unconstrained. There is none other God but Thee, the God of love and tender mercy, the All-Glorious, the Ever-Forgiving.

—'Abdu'l-Bahá

"(in the) Síyáh-Chál...We were placed in two rows, each facing the other. We had taught them to repeat certain verses which, every night, they chanted ...

'God is sufficient unto me; He verily is the All-sufficing!' one row would intone, while the other would reply: 'In Him let the trusting trust." —Bahá'u'lláh

MEETINGS

Glorified art Thou, O Lord my God! I implore Thee by the onrushing winds of Thy grace, and by them Who are the Daysprings of Thy purpose and the Dawning-Places of Thine inspiration, to send down upon me and upon all that have sought Thy face that which beseemeth Thy generosity and bountiful grace, and is worthy of Thy bestowals and favors. Poor and desolate I am, O my Lord! Immerse me in the ocean of Thy wealth; athirst, suffer me to drink from the living waters of Thy loving-kindness.

I beseech Thee, by Thine own Self and by Him Whom Thou hast appointed as the Manifestation of Thine own Being and Thy discriminating Word unto all that are in heaven and on earth, to gather together Thy servants beneath the shade of the Tree of Thy gracious providence. Help them, then, to partake of its fruits, to incline their ears to the rustling of its leaves, and to the sweetness of the voice of the Bird that chanteth upon its branches. Thou art, verily, the Help in Peril, the Inaccessible, the Almighty, the Most Bountiful. —Bahá'u'lláh

O God! Verily, we have gathered here in the fragrance of Thy love. We have turned to Thy Kingdom. We seek naught save Thee and desire nothing save Thy good pleasure. O God! Let this food be Thy manna from heaven, and grant that this assemblage may be a concourse of Thy supreme ones. May they be the quickening cause of love to humanity and the source of illumination to the human race. May they be the instruments of Thy guidance upon earth. Verily, Thou art powerful. Thou art the Bestower. Thou art the Forgiver, and Thou art the Almighty.

—'Abdu'l-Bahá

O Divine Providence! This assemblage is composed of Thy friends who are attracted to Thy beauty and are set ablaze by the fire of Thy love. Turn these souls into heavenly angels, resuscitate them through the breath of Thy Holy Spirit, grant them eloquent tongues and resolute hearts, bestow upon them heavenly power and merciful susceptibilities, cause them to become the promulgators of the oneness of mankind and the cause of love and concord in the world of humanity, so that the perilous darkness of ignorant prejudice may vanish through the light of the Sun of Truth, this dreary world may become illumined, this material realm may absorb the rays of the world of spirit, these different colors may merge into one color and the melody of praise may rise to the kingdom of Thy sanctity. Verily, Thou art the Omnipotent and the Almighty! —'Abdu'l-Bahá

"They who are the beloved of God, in whatever place they gather and whomsoever they may meet, must evince, in their attitude towards God, and in the manner of their celebration of His praise and glory, such humility and submissiveness that every atom of the dust beneath their feet may attest the depth of their devotion. The conversation carried by these holy souls should be informed with such power that these same atoms of dust will be thrilled by its influence." —Bahá'u'lláh

MORNING

"Occupy thyself in remembrance of the Beauty of Him Who is the Unconstrained at early morn, and seek communion with Him at the hour of dawn..."

—Bahá'u'lláh

O my God and my Master! I am Thy servant and the son of Thy servant. I have risen from my couch at this dawn-tide when the Daystar of Thy oneness hath shone forth from the Dayspring of Thy will, and hath shed its radiance upon the whole world, according to what had been ordained in the Books of Thy Decree.

Praise be unto Thee, O my God, that we have wakened to the splendors of the light of Thy knowledge. Send down, then, upon us, O my Lord, what will enable us to dispense with anyone but Thee, and will rid us of all attachment to aught except Thyself. Write down, moreover, for me, and for such as are dear to me, and for my kindred, man and woman alike, the good of this world and the world to come. Keep us safe, then, through Thine unfailing protection, O Thou the Beloved of the entire creation and the Desire of the whole universe, from them whom Thou hast made to be the manifestations of the Evil Whisperer, who whisper in men's breasts. Potent art Thou to do Thy pleasure. Thou art, verily, the Almighty, the Help in Peril, the Self-Subsisting.

Bless Thou, O Lord my God, Him Whom Thou hast set over Thy most excellent Titles, and through Whom Thou hast divided between the godly and the wicked, and graciously aid us to do what Thou lovest and desirest. Bless Thou, moreover, O my God, them Who are Thy Words and Thy Letters, and them who have set their faces towards Thee, and turned unto Thy face, and hearkened to Thy Call.

Thou art, truly, the Lord and King of all men, and art potent over all things. —Bahá'u'lláh

I have wakened in Thy shelter, O my God, and it becometh him that seeketh that shelter to abide within the Sanctuary of Thy protection and the Stronghold of Thy defense. Illumine my inner being, O my Lord, with the splendors of the Dayspring of Thy Revelation, even as Thou didst illumine my outer being with the morning light of Thy favor.

—Bahá'u'lláh

NATIONS

O Lord! Bestow Thy gracious aid and confirmation upon this just government. This country lieth beneath the sheltering shadow of Thy protection, and this people is in Thy service. O Lord! Confer upon them Thy heavenly bounty and render the outpourings of Thy grace and favor copious and abundant. Suffer this esteemed nation to be held in honor, and enable it to be admitted into Thy kingdom.

Thou art the Powerful, the Omnipotent, the Merciful, and Thou art the Generous, the Beneficent, the Lord of grace abounding. —'Abdu'l-Bahá

"Blessed and happy is he that ariseth to promote the best interests of the peoples and kindreds of the earth...It is not for him to pride himself who loveth his own country, but rather for him who loveth the whole world. The earth is but one country, and mankind its citizens." —Bahá'u'lláh

NIGHT

O my God, my Master, the Goal of my desire! This, Thy servant, seeketh to sleep in the shelter of Thy mercy, and to repose beneath the canopy of Thy grace, imploring Thy care and Thy protection.

I beg of Thee, O my Lord, by Thine eye that sleepeth not, to guard mine eyes from beholding aught beside Thee. Strengthen, then, their vision that they may discern Thy signs, and behold the Horizon of Thy Revelation. Thou art He before the revelations of Whose omnipotence the quintessence of power hath trembled. No God is there but Thee, the Almighty, the All-Subduing, the Unconditioned.

—Bahá'u'lláh

How can I choose to sleep, O God, my God, when the eyes of them that long for Thee are wakeful because of their separation from Thee; and how can I lie down to rest whilst the souls of Thy lovers are sore vexed in their remoteness from Thy presence?

I have committed, O my Lord, my spirit and my entire being into the right hand of Thy might and Thy protection, and I lay my head on my pillow through Thy power, and lift it up according to Thy will and

Thy good pleasure. Thou art, in truth, the Preserver, the Keeper, the Almighty, the Most Powerful.

By Thy might! I ask not, whether sleeping or waking, but that which Thou dost desire. I am Thy servant and in Thy hands. Do Thou graciously aid me to do what will shed forth the fragrance of Thy good pleasure. This, truly, is my hope and the hope of them that enjoy near access to Thee. Praised be Thou, O Lord of the worlds! —Bahá'u'lláh

MIDNIGHT

O seeker of Truth! If thou desirest that God may open thine eye, thou must supplicate unto God, pray to and commune with Him at midnight, saying:

O Lord, I have turned my face unto Thy kingdom of oneness and am immersed in the sea of Thy mercy. O Lord, enlighten my sight by beholding Thy lights in this dark night, and make me happy by the wine of Thy love in this wonderful age. O Lord, make me hear Thy call, and open before my face the doors of Thy heaven, so that I may see the light of Thy glory and become attracted to Thy beauty. Verily, Thou art the Giver, the Generous, the Merciful, the Forgiving. —'Abdu'l-Bahá

PARENTS

Thou seest, O Lord, our suppliant hands lifted up towards the heaven of Thy favor and bounty. Grant that they may be filled with the treasures of Thy munificence and bountiful favor. Forgive us, and our fathers, and our mothers, and fulfill whatsoever we have desired from the ocean of Thy grace and Divine generosity. Accept, O Beloved of our hearts, all our works in Thy path. Thou art, verily, the Most Powerful, the Most Exalted, the Incomparable, the One, the Forgiving, the Gracious.

—Bahá'u'lláh

O Lord! In this Most Great Dispensation Thou dost accept the intercession of children in behalf of their parents. This is one of the special infinite bestowals of this Dispensation. Therefore, O Thou kind Lord, accept the request of this Thy servant at the threshold of Thy singleness and submerge his father in the ocean of Thy grace, because this son hath risen to render Thee service and is exerting effort at all times in the pathway of Thy love. Verily, Thou art the Giver, the Forgiver and the Kind!

—'Abdu'l-Bahá

"It is seemly that the servant should, after each prayer, supplicate God to bestow mercy and forgiveness upon his parents. Thereupon God's call will be raised: 'Thousand upon thousand of what thou hast asked for thy parents shall be thy recompense!' Blessed is he who remembereth his parents when communing with God. There is, verily, no God but Him, the Mighty, the Well-Beloved." —The Báb

"Likewise, parents endure the greatest toil and trouble for their children, and often, by the time the latter have reached the age of maturity, the former have hastened to the world beyond. Rarely do the mother and father enjoy in this world the rewards of all the pain and trouble they have endured for their children. The children must therefore, in return for this pain and trouble, make charitable contributions and perform good works in their name, and implore pardon and forgiveness for their souls. You should therefore, in return for the love and kindness of your father, give to the poor in his name and, with the utmost lowliness and fervor, pray for God's pardon and forgiveness and seek His infinite mercy."

—'Abdu'l-Bahá

PIONEERS

Thou knowest, O God, and art my witness, that I have no desire in my heart save to attain Thy good pleasure, to be confirmed in servitude to Thee, to consecrate myself in Thy service, to labor in Thy great vineyard and to sacrifice all in thy path. Thou art the All-Knowing and the All-Seeing. I have no wish save to turn my steps, in my love for thee, towards the mountains and the deserts, to loudly proclaim the advent of Thy Kingdom, and to raise Thy call amidst all men. O God! Open Thou the way for this helpless one, grant Thou the remedy to this ailing one and bestow Thy healing upon this afflicted one. With burning heart and tearful eyes I supplicate Thee at Thy Threshold. O God! I am prepared to endure any ordeal in Thy path and desire with all my heart and soul to meet any hardship.

O God! Protect me from tests. Thou knowest full well that I have turned away from all things and freed myself of all thoughts. I have no occupation save mention of Thee and no aspiration save serving Thee.

—'Abdu'l-Bahá

PRAISE AND GRATITUDE

All praise, O my God, be to Thee Who art the Source of all glory and majesty, of greatness and honor, of sovereignty and dominion, of loftiness and grace, of awe and power. Whomsoever Thou willest Thou causest to draw nigh unto the Most Great Ocean, and on whomsoever Thou desirest Thou conferrest the honor of recognizing Thy Most Ancient Name. Of all who are in heaven and on earth, none can withstand the operation of Thy sovereign Will. From all eternity Thou didst rule the entire creation, and Thou wilt continue for evermore to exercise Thy dominion over all created things. There is none other God but Thee, the Almighty, The Most Exalted, the All-Powerful, the All-Wise.

Illumine, O Lord, the faces of Thy servants, that they may behold Thee; and cleanse their hearts that they may turn unto the court of Thy heavenly favors, and recognize Him Who is the Manifestation of Thy Self and the Dayspring of Thine Essence. Verily, Thou art the Lord of all worlds. There is no God but Thee, the Unconstrained, the All-Subduing.

—Bahá'u'lláh

O compassionate God! Thanks be to Thee for Thou hast awakened and made me conscious. Thou hast given me a seeing eye and favored me with a hearing ear, hast led me to Thy kingdom and guided me to Thy path. Thou hast shown me the right way and caused me to enter the ark of deliverance. O God! Keep me steadfast and make me firm and staunch. Protect me from violent tests and preserve and shelter me in the strongly fortified fortress of Thy Covenant and Testament. Thou art the Powerful. Thou art the Seeing. Thou art the Hearing.

O Thou the Compassionate God. Bestow upon me a heart which, like unto a glass, may be illumined with the light of Thy love, and confer upon me thoughts which may change this world into a rose garden through the outpourings of heavenly grace. Thou art the Compassionate, the Merciful. Thou art the Great Beneficent God.

—'Abdu'l-Bahá

PROTECTION

"If thou desirest to be freed from affliction, recite thou this prayer which hath been revealed by the Pen of the All-Merciful:

O God, my God! I testify to Thy unity and to Thy oneness. I beseech Thee, O Thou Possessor of names and Fashioner of the heavens, by the pervasive influence of Thine exalted Word and the potency of Thy supreme Pen, to aid me with the ensigns of Thy power and might, and to protect me from the mischief of Thine enemies who have violated Thy Covenant and Thy Testament. Thou art, verily, the Almighty, the Most Powerful.

This invocation (above) is an impregnable stronghold and an indomitable army. It conferreth protection and ensureth deliverance."

—Bahá'u'lláh

In His Name, the Exalted, the All-Highest, the Most Sublime! Glorified art Thou, O Lord my God! O Thou Who art my God, and my Master, and my Lord, and my Support, and my Hope, and my Refuge, and my Light. I ask of Thee, by Thy

Hidden and Treasured Name, that none knoweth save Thine own Self, to protect the bearer of this Tablet from every calamity and pestilence, and from every wicked man and woman; from the evil of the evil-doers, and from the scheming of the unbelievers. Preserve him, moreover, O my God, from every pain and vexation, O Thou Who holdest in Thy hand the empire of all things. Thou, truly, art powerful over all things. Thou doest as Thou willest, and ordainest as Thou pleasest.

O Thou King of Kings! O Thou kind Lord! O Thou Source of ancient bounty, of grace, of generosity and bestowal! O Thou Healer of sicknesses! O Thou Sufficer of needs! O Thou Light of Light! O Thou Light above all Lights! O Thou Revealer of every Manifestation! O Thou the Compassionate! O Thou the Merciful! Do Thou have mercy upon the bearer of this Tablet, through Thy most great mercy and Thine abundant grace, O Thou the Gracious, Thou the Bounteous. Guard him, moreover, through Thy protection, from whatsoever his heart and mind may find repugnant. Of those endued with power, Thou, verily, art the most powerful. The Glory of

God rest upon thee, O thou rising sun! Do thou testify unto that which God hath testified of His own Self, that there is none other God besides Him, the Almighty, the Best-Beloved.

—Bahá'u'lláh

Lauded be Thy name, O Lord my God! I entreat Thee by Thy Name through which the Hour hath struck, and the Resurrection came to pass, and fear and trembling seized all that are in heaven and all that are on earth, to rain down, out of the heaven of Thy mercy and the clouds of Thy tender compassion, what will gladden the hearts of Thy servants, who have turned towards Thee and helped Thy Cause.

Keep safe Thy servants and Thy handmaidens, O my Lord, from the darts of idle fancy and vain imaginings, and give them from the hands of Thy grace a draught of the soft-flowing waters of Thy knowledge. Thou, truly, art the Almighty, the Most Exalted, the Ever-Forgiving, the Most Generous.

—Bahá'u'lláh

O God, my God! Shield Thy trusted servants from the evils of self and passion, protect them with the watchful eye of Thy loving-kindness from all rancor, hate and envy, shelter them in the impregnable stronghold of Thy care and, safe from the darts of doubtfulness, make them the manifestations of Thy glorious signs, illumine their faces with the effulgent rays shed from the Dayspring of Thy divine unity, gladden their hearts with the verses revealed from Thy holy kingdom, strengthen their loins by Thine all-swaying power that cometh from Thy realm of glory. Thou art the All-Bountiful, the Protector, the Almighty, the Gracious.

—'Abdu'l-Bahá

He is the Compassionate, the All-Bountiful! O God, my God! Thou seest me, Thou knowest me; Thou art my Haven and my Refuge. None have I sought nor any will I seek save Thee; no path have I trodden nor any will I tread but the path of Thy love. In the darksome night of despair, my eye turneth expectant and full of hope to the morn of Thy boundless favor and at the hour of dawn my drooping soul is refreshed and strengthened in remembrance of Thy beauty and perfection. He whom the grace of Thy mercy aideth, though he be but a drop, shall become the boundless ocean, and the merest atom which the outpouring of Thy loving-kindness assisteth, shall shine even as the radiant star.

Shelter under Thy protection, O Thou Spirit of purity, Thou Who art the All-Bountiful Provider, this enthralled, enkindled servant of Thine. Aid him in this world of being to remain steadfast and firm in Thy love and grant that this broken-winged bird attain a refuge and shelter in Thy divine nest that abideth upon the celestial tree.

—'Abdu'l-Bahá

O Thou divine Providence, preserve and protect us! O Thou Who art our Shield, save us and defend us! Keep us beneath Thy Shelter, and by Thy Help save us from all ills. Thou art, indeed, the True Protector, the Unseen Guardian, the Celestial Preserver, and the Heavenly Loving Lord.

—'Abdu'l-Bahá

PURITY & CLEANLINESS

O Divine Providence! Bestow Thou in all things purity and cleanliness upon the people of Bahá. Grant that they be freed from all defilement, and released from all addictions. Save them from committing any repugnant act, unbind them from the chains of every evil habit, that they may live pure and free, wholesome and cleanly, worthy to serve at Thy Sacred Threshold and fit to be related to their Lord.

—'Abdu'l-Bahá

"Make ye then a mighty effort, that the purity and sanctity which, above all else, are cherished by 'Abdu'l-Bahá, shall distinguish the people of Bahá... that for purity, immaculacy, refinement, and the preservation of health, they shall be leaders in the vanguard... And that by their freedom from enslavement, their knowledge, their self-control, they shall be first among the pure, the free and the wise."

—'Abdu'l-Bahá

THE SPIRITUAL ASSEMBLY

Whenever ye enter the council-chamber, recite this prayer with a heart throbbing with the love of God and a tongue purified from all but His remembrance, that the All-Powerful may graciously aid you to achieve supreme victory.

O God, my God! We are servants of Thine that have turned with devotion to Thy Holy Face, that have detached ourselves from all besides Thee in this glorious Day. We have gathered in this Spiritual Assembly, united in our views and thoughts, with our purposes harmonized to exalt Thy Word amidst mankind.

O Lord, our God! Make us the signs of Thy Divine Guidance, the Standards of Thine exalted Faith amongst men, servants to Thy mighty Covenant, O Thou our Lord Most High, manifestations of Thy Divine Unity in Thine Abhá Kingdom, and resplendent stars shining upon all regions. Lord! Aid us to become seas surging with the billows of Thy wondrous Grace, streams flowing from Thine all-glorious Heights, goodly fruits upon the Tree of Thy heavenly Cause, trees waving through the breezes of Thy Bounty in Thy celestial Vineyard. O God! Make our souls dependent upon the Verses of Thy Divine Unity, our hearts cheered with the outpourings of Thy Grace, that we may unite even as the waves of one sea and become merged together as the rays of Thine effulgent Light; that our thoughts, our views, our feelings may become as one reality, manifesting the spirit of union throughout the world. Thou art the Gracious, the Bountiful, the Bestower, the Almighty, the Merciful, the Compassionate. —'Abdu'l-Bahá

Come ye together in gladness unalloyed, and at the beginning of the meeting, recite ye this prayer:

O Thou Lord of the Kingdom! Though our bodies be gathered here together, yet our spellbound hearts are carried away by Thy love, and yet are we transported by the rays of Thy resplendent face. Weak though we be, we await the revelations of Thy might and power. Poor though we be, with neither goods nor means, still take we riches from the treasures of Thy Kingdom. Drops though we be, still do we draw from out Thy ocean deeps.

Motes though we be, still do we gleam in the glory of Thy splendid Sun. O Thou our Provider! Send down Thine aid, that each one gathered here may become a lighted candle, each one a center of attraction, each one a summoner to Thy heavenly realms, till at last we make this nether world the mirror image of Thy Paradise. —'Abdu'l-Bahá

Prayer to be said at the close of the meeting of the Spiritual Assembly.

O God! O God! From the unseen kingdom of Thy oneness behold us assembled in this spiritual meeting, believing in Thee, confident in Thy signs, firm in Thy Covenant and Testament, attracted to Thee, set aglow with the fire of Thy love and sincere in Thy Cause. We are servants in Thy vineyard, spreaders of Thy religion, devoted worshipers of Thy countenance, humble towards Thy loved ones, submissive before Thy door, and imploring Thee to confirm us in serving Thy chosen ones, to support us with Thine unseen hosts, to strengthen our loins in Thy servitude and to make us submissive and adoring subjects communing with Thee.

O our Lord! We are weak, and Thou art the Mighty, the Powerful. We are lifeless, and Thou art the great life-giving Spirit. We are needy, and Thou art the Sustainer, the Powerful.

O our Lord! Turn our faces unto Thy merciful countenance, feed us from Thy heavenly table with Thine abundant grace, assist us with the hosts of Thy supreme angels and confirm us through the holy ones of the Kingdom of Abhá.

Verily, Thou art the Generous, the Merciful. Thou art the Possessor of great bounty, and, verily, Thou art the Clement and the Gracious.

—'Abdu'l-Bahá

"Take ye counsel together in all matters, inasmuch as consultation is the lamp of guidance which leadeth the way, and is the bestower of understanding."

—Bahá'u'lláh

SPIRITUAL GROWTH

My God, my Adored One, my King, my Desire! What tongue can voice my thanks to Thee? I was heedless, Thou didst awaken me. I had turned back from Thee, Thou didst graciously aid me to turn towards Thee. I was as one dead, Thou didst quicken me with the water of life. I was withered, Thou didst revive me with the heavenly stream of Thine utterance which hath flowed forth from the Pen of the All-Merciful.

O Divine Providence! All existence is begotten by Thy bounty; deprive it not of the waters of Thy generosity, neither do Thou withhold it from the ocean of Thy mercy. I beseech Thee to aid and assist me at all times and under all conditions, and seek from the heaven of Thy grace Thine ancient favor. Thou art, in truth, the Lord of bounty, and the Sovereign of the kingdom of eternity.

—Bahá'u'lláh

Do Thou ordain for me through Thy most exalted pen, O my Lord, the good of this world and of the next. I testify that within Thy grasp are held the reins of all things. Thou changest them as Thou pleasest. No God is there save Thee, the Strong, the Faithful.

Thou art He Who changeth through His bidding, abasement into glory, and weakness into strength, and powerlessness into might, and fear into calm, and doubt into certainty. No God is there but Thee, the Mighty, the Beneficent.

Thou disappointest no one who hath sought Thee, nor dost Thou keep back from Thee anyone who hath desired Thee. Ordain Thou for me what becometh the heaven of Thy generosity, and the ocean of Thy bounty. Thou art, verily, the Almighty, the Most Powerful. —Bahá'u'lláh

I beseech Thee, O my God, by all the transcendent glory of Thy Name, to clothe Thy loved ones in the robe of justice and to illumine their beings with the light of trustworthiness.

Thou art the One that hath power to do as He pleaseth and Who holdeth within His grasp the reins of all things, visible and invisible.

—Bahá'u'lláh

O Lord! We are weak; strengthen us. O God! We are ignorant; make us knowing. O Lord! We are poor; make us wealthy. O God! We are dead; quicken us. O Lord! We are humiliation itself; glorify us in Thy Kingdom. If Thou dost assist us, O Lord, we shall become as scintillating stars. If Thou dost not assist us, we shall become lower than the earth.

O Lord! Strengthen us. O God! Confer victory upon us. O God! Enable us to conquer self and overcome desire. O Lord! Deliver us from the bondage of the material world. O Lord! Quicken us through the breath of the Holy Spirit in order that we may arise to serve Thee, engage in worshiping Thee and exert ourselves in Thy Kingdom with the utmost sincerity. O Lord, Thou art Powerful. O God, Thou art Forgiving. O Lord, Thou art Compassionate.

—'Abdu'l-Bahá

TEACHING

"Teach thou the Cause of God with an utterance which will cause the bushes to be enkindled, and the call 'Verily, there is no God but Me, the Almighty, the Unconstrained' to be raised therefrom."

—Bahá'u'lláh

Lauded be Thy name, O Lord my God! Thou beholdest how my gaze is fixed toward Thy tender mercies, and how mine eyes are bent upon the horizon of Thy grace, and Thy loving-kindness, and how my hands are stretched out unto the heaven of Thy bestowals.

Thy might beareth me witness! Every limb of my body crieth out to Thee and saith: "O Thou Who art the Well-Beloved of the worlds, and the Lord of all that are in heaven and on earth, and the one Desire of the hearts which are devoted to Thee! I implore Thee, by Thine Ocean unto which Thou didst summon all the inmates of heaven and all the dwellers of the earth, to help Thy servants who have been kept back from turning unto it and from approaching its shores. Make them, then, O my God, to be detached from all else but Thee, and enable them to speak forth Thy praise and extol Thy virtues. Supply them, moreover, O my God, with the choice Wine of Thy mercy, that it may cause them to be forgetful of any one except Thee, and to arise to serve Thy Cause, and to be steadfast in their love for Thee. Thou art, verily, the Lord of their lives and the Object of their adoration.

If they be driven away by Thee, who will then look upon them; and if they be removed far from Thee, who is there that can help them to approach Thy Presence? I swear by Thy might! No refuge is there to flee to except Thee, and no shelter to seek except Thy shelter, and no protection except Thy protection. Woe betide him who hath taken as Lord any one beside Thee, and blessed are the ones who have rid themselves of all attachment to all the dwellers of Thine earth, and clung to the hem of Thy bounteousness. These! the people of Bahá, before all that are in heaven and all that are on earth. No God is there but Thee, the Omniscient, the All-Wise." Praise be to God, the Lord of all worlds.

—Bahá'u'lláh

O my God, aid Thou Thy servant to raise up the Word, and to refute what is vain and false, to establish the truth, to spread the sacred verses abroad, reveal the splendors, and make the morning's light to dawn in the hearts of the righteous. Thou art, verily, the Generous, the Forgiving. —'Abdu'l-Bahá

The following commune to be read… every day:

O God! O God! This is a broken-winged bird and his flight is very slow – assist him so that he may fly toward the apex of prosperity and salvation, wing his way with the utmost joy and happiness throughout the illimitable space, raise his melody in Thy Supreme Name in all the regions, exhilarate the ears with this call, and brighten the eyes by beholding the signs of guidance.

O Lord! I am single, alone and lowly. For me there is no support save Thee, no helper except Thee and no sustainer beside Thee. Confirm me in Thy service, assist me with the cohorts of Thy angels, make me victorious in the promotion of Thy Word and suffer me to speak out Thy wisdom amongst Thy creatures. Verily, Thou art the helper of the weak and the defender of the little ones, and verily Thou art the Powerful, the Mighty and the Unconstrained. —'Abdu'l-Bahá

O Thou incomparable God! O Thou Lord of the Kingdom! These souls are Thy heavenly army. Assist them and, with the cohorts of the Supreme Concourse, make them victorious, so that each one of them may become like unto a regiment and conquer these countries through the love of God and the illumination of divine teachings.

O God! Be Thou their supporter and their helper, and in the wilderness, the mountain, the valley, the forests, the prairies and the seas, be Thou their confidant—so that they may cry out through the power of the Kingdom and the breath of the Holy Spirit.

Verily, Thou art the Powerful, the Mighty and the Omnipotent, and Thou art the Wise, the Hearing and the Seeing. —'Abdu'l-Bahá

O God, my God! Aid Thou Thy trusted servants to have loving and tender hearts. Help them to spread, amongst all the nations of the earth, the light of guidance that cometh from the Company on high. Verily, Thou art the Strong, the Powerful, the Mighty, the All-Subduing, the Ever-Giving. Verily, Thou art the Generous, the Gentle, the Tender, the Most Bountiful. —'Abdu'l-Bahá

"The source of courage and power is the promotion of the Word of God, and steadfastness in His Love."

"O Son of Being! Make mention of Me on My earth, that in My heaven I may remember thee, thus shall Mine eyes and thine be solaced." —Bahá'u'lláh

TESTS AND DIFFICULTIES

Dispel my grief by Thy bounty and Thy generosity, O God, my God, and banish mine anguish through Thy sovereignty and Thy might. Thou seest me, O my God, with my face set towards Thee at a time when sorrows have compassed me on every side. I implore Thee, O Thou Who art the Lord of all being, and overshadowest all things visible and invisible, by Thy Name whereby Thou hast subdued the hearts and the souls of men, and by the billows of the Ocean of Thy mercy and the splendors of the Daystar of Thy bounty, to number me with them whom nothing whatsoever hath deterred from setting their faces toward Thee, O Thou Lord of all names and Maker of the heavens!

Thou beholdest, O my Lord, the things which have befallen me in Thy days. I entreat Thee, by Him Who is the Dayspring of Thy names and the Dawning-Place of Thine attributes, to ordain for me what will enable me to arise to serve Thee and to extol Thy virtues. Thou art, verily, the Almighty, the Most Powerful, Who art wont to answer the prayers of all men!

And, finally, I beg of Thee by the light of Thy countenance to bless my affairs, and redeem my debts, and satisfy my needs. Thou art He to Whose power and to Whose dominion every tongue hath testified, and Whose majesty and Whose sovereignty every understanding heart hath acknowledged. No God is there but Thee, Who hearest and art ready to answer. —Bahá'u'lláh

I adjure Thee by Thy might, O my God! Let no harm beset me in times of tests, and in moments of heedlessness guide my steps aright through Thine inspiration. Thou art God, potent art Thou to do what Thou desirest. No one can withstand Thy Will or thwart Thy Purpose. —The Báb

O Lord! Thou art the Remover of every anguish and the Dispeller of every affliction. Thou art He Who banisheth every sorrow and setteth free every slave, the Redeemer of every soul.

O Lord! Grant deliverance through Thy mercy, and reckon me among such servants of Thine as have gained salvation. —The Báb

O my Lord! Thou knowest that the people are encircled with pain and calamities and are environed with hardships and trouble. Every trial doth attack man and every dire adversity doth assail him like unto the assault of a serpent. There is no shelter and asylum for him except under the wing of Thy protection, preservation, guard and custody.

O Thou the Merciful One! O my Lord! Make Thy protection my armor, Thy preservation my shield, humbleness before the door of Thy oneness my guard, and Thy custody and defense my fortress and my abode. Preserve me from the suggestions of self and desire, and guard me from every sickness, trial, difficulty and ordeal.

Verily, Thou art the Protector, the Guardian, the Preserver, the Sufficer, and verily, Thou art the Merciful of the Most Merciful. —'Abdu'l-Bahá

O Lord, my God and my Haven in my distress! My Shield and my Shelter in my woes! My Asylum and Refuge in time of need and in my loneliness my Companion! In my anguish my Solace, and in my solitude a loving Friend!

The Remover of the pangs of my sorrows and the Pardoner of my sins! Wholly unto Thee do I turn, fervently imploring Thee with all my heart, my mind and my tongue, to shield me from all that runs counter to Thy will in this, the cycle of Thy divine unity, and to cleanse me of all defilement that will hinder me from seeking, stainless and unsullied, the shade of the tree of Thy grace.

Have mercy, O Lord, on the feeble, make whole the sick, and quench the burning thirst. Gladden the bosom wherein the fire of Thy love doth smolder, and set it aglow with the flame of Thy celestial love and spirit.

Robe the tabernacles of divine unity with the vesture of holiness, and set upon my head the crown of Thy favor. Illumine my face with the radiance of the orb of Thy bounty, and graciously aid me in ministering at Thy holy threshold.

Make my heart overflow with love for Thy creatures and grant that I may become the sign of Thy mercy, the token of Thy grace, the promoter of concord amongst Thy loved ones, devoted unto Thee, uttering Thy commemoration and forgetful of self but ever mindful of what is Thine.

O God, my God! Stay not from me the gentle gales of Thy pardon and grace, and deprive me not of the wellsprings of Thine aid and favor. 'Neath the shade of Thy protecting wings let me nestle, and cast upon me the glance of Thine all-protecting eye.

Loose my tongue to laud Thy name amidst Thy people, that my voice may be raised in great assemblies and from my lips may stream the flood of Thy praise. Thou art, in all truth, the Gracious, the Glorified, the Mighty, the Omnipotent.

—'Abdu'l-Bahá

"Armed with the power of Thy name nothing can ever hurt me, and with Thy love in my heart all the world's afflictions can in no wise alarm me."

—Bahá'u'lláh

UNITY

God grant that the light of unity may envelop the whole earth, and that the seal, "the Kingdom is God's", may be stamped upon the brow of all its peoples. —Bahá'u'lláh

Glory be to Thee, O God, for Thy manifestation of love to mankind! O Thou Who art our Life and Light, guide Thy servants in Thy way, and make us rich in Thee and free from all save Thee.

O God, teach us Thy Oneness and give us a realization of Thy Unity, that we may see no one save Thee. Thou art the Merciful and the Giver of bounty!

O God, create in the hearts of Thy beloved the fire of Thy love, that it may consume the thought of everything save Thee.

Reveal to us, O God, Thine exalted eternity - that Thou hast ever been and wilt ever be, and that there is no God save Thee. Verily, in Thee will we find comfort and strength. —Bahá'u'lláh

O my God! O my God! Unite the hearts of Thy servants, and reveal to them Thy great purpose. May they follow Thy commandments and abide in Thy law. Help them, O God, in their endeavor, and grant them strength to serve Thee. O God! Leave them not to themselves, but guide their steps by the light of Thy knowledge, and cheer their hearts by Thy love. Verily, Thou art their Helper and their Lord.

—Bahá'u'lláh

O Thou Who art the Lord of Lords! I testify that Thou art the Lord of all creation, and the Educator of all beings, visible and invisible. I bear witness that Thy power hath encompassed the entire universe, and that the hosts of the earth can never dismay Thee, nor can the dominion of all peoples and nations deter Thee from executing Thy purpose. I confess that Thou hast no desire except the regeneration of the whole world, and the establishment of the unity of its peoples, and the salvation of all them that dwell therein.

—Bahá'u'lláh

WOMEN

I am, O my Lord, Thy handmaiden, who hath hearkened to Thy call, and hastened unto Thee, fleeing from herself and resting her heart upon Thee. I implore Thee, O my Lord, by Thy name out of which all the treasures of the earth were brought forth, to shield me from the hints of such as have disbelieved in Thee and repudiated Thy truth. Powerful art Thou to do what Thou pleasest. Thou art, verily, the All-Knowing, the All-Wise.

—Bahá'u'lláh

O Thou kind Lord! Bestow heavenly confirmation upon this daughter of the kingdom, and graciously aid her that she may remain firm and steadfast in Thy Cause and that she may, even as a nightingale of the rose garden of mysteries, warble melodies in the Abhá Kingdom in the most wondrous tones, thereby bringing happiness to everyone. Make her exalted among the daughters of the kingdom and enable her to attain life eternal. Thou art the Bestower, the All-Loving.

—'Abdu'l-Bahá

O my Lord, my Beloved, my Desire! Befriend me in my loneliness and accompany me in my exile. Remove my sorrow. Cause me to be devoted to Thy beauty. Withdraw me from all else save Thee. Attract me through Thy fragrances of holiness. Cause me to be associated in Thy Kingdom with those who are severed from all else save Thee, who long to serve Thy sacred threshold and who stand to work in Thy Cause. Enable me to be one of Thy maidservants who have attained to Thy good pleasure. Verily, Thou art the Gracious, the Generous. —'Abdu'l-Bahá

FOR EXPECTANT MOTHERS

My Lord! My Lord! I praise Thee and I thank Thee for that whereby Thou hast favored Thine humble maidservant, Thy slave beseeching and supplicating Thee, because Thou hast verily guided her unto Thine obvious Kingdom and caused her to hear Thine exalted Call in the contingent world and to behold Thy Signs which prove the appearance of Thy victorious reign over all things. O my Lord, I dedicate that which is in my womb unto Thee. Then, cause it to be a praiseworthy child in Thy Kingdom and a fortunate one by Thy favor and Thy generosity; to develop and to grow up under the charge of Thine education. Verily, Thou art the Gracious! Verily, Thou art the Lord of Great Favor!

—'Abdu'l-Bahá

"O maid-servants of the merciful! It is incumbent upon you to train the children from their earliest babyhood! It is incumbent upon you to beautify their morals! It is incumbent upon you to attend to them under all aspects and circumstances, inasmuch as God – glorified and exalted is He! – hath ordained mothers to be the primary trainers of children and infants. This is a great and important affair and a high and exalted position, and it is not allowable to slacken therein at all!"

—'Abdu'l-Bahá

YOUTH

O Lord! Make this youth radiant, and confer Thy bounty upon this poor creature. Bestow upon him knowledge, grant him added strength at the break of every morn and guard him within the shelter of Thy protection so that he may be freed from error, may devote himself to the service of Thy Cause, may guide the wayward, lead the hapless, free the captives and awaken the heedless, that all may be blessed with Thy remembrance and praise. Thou art the Mighty and the Powerful.

—'Abdu'l-Bahá

O Thou kind Lord! Graciously bestow a pair of heavenly wings unto each of these fledglings, and give them spiritual power that they may wing their flight through this limitless space and may soar to the heights of the Abhá Kingdom.

O Lord! Strengthen these fragile seedlings that each one may become a fruitful tree, verdant and flourishing. Render these souls victorious through the potency of Thy celestial hosts, that they may be able to crush the forces of error and ignorance and to unfurl the standard of fellowship and guidance amidst the people; that they may, even as the reviving breaths of spring, refresh and quicken the trees of human souls and like unto vernal showers make the meads of that region green and fertile.

Thou art the Mighty and the Powerful; Thou art the Bestower and the All-Loving.

—'Abdu'l-Bahá

O Thou kind Lord! Grant that this youth may attain unto that which is the highest aspiration of the holy ones. Endow him with the wings of Thy strengthening grace - wings of detachment and divine aid - that he may soar thereby into the atmosphere of Thy tender mercy, be able to partake of Thy celestial bestowals, may become a sign of divine guidance and a standard of the Concourse on high. Thou art the Potent, the Powerful, the Seeing, the Hearing.

—'Abdu'l-Bahá

OCCASIONAL PRAYERS & SPECIAL TABLETS

AYYÁM-I-HÁ

The Days of Há (The Intercalary Days) – February to March[1] should be days of preparation for the Fast, days of hospitality, charity and giving of gifts.

My God, my Fire and my Light! The days which Thou hast named the Ayyám-i-Há in Thy Book have begun, O Thou Who art the King of names, and the fast which Thy most exalted Pen hath enjoined unto all who are in the kingdom of Thy creation to observe is approaching. I entreat Thee, O my Lord, by these days and by all such as have during that period clung to the cord of Thy commandments, and laid hold on the handle of Thy precepts, to grant that unto every soul may be assigned a place within the precincts of Thy court, and a seat at the revelation of the splendors of the light of Thy countenance.

These, O my Lord, are Thy servants whom no

1 Refer to the Badí' Calendar for the exact date.

corrupt inclination hath kept back from what Thou didst send down in Thy Book. They have bowed themselves before Thy Cause, and received Thy Book with such resolve as is born of Thee, and observed what Thou hadst prescribed unto them, and chosen to follow that which had been sent down by Thee.

Thou seest, O my Lord, how they have recognized and confessed whatsoever Thou hast revealed in Thy Scriptures. Give them to drink, O my Lord, from the hands of Thy graciousness the waters of Thine eternity. Write down, then, for them the recompense ordained for him that hath immersed himself in the ocean of Thy presence, and attained unto the choice wine of Thy meeting.

I implore Thee, O Thou the King of kings and the Pitier of the downtrodden, to ordain for them the good of this world and of the world to come. Write down for them, moreover, what none of Thy creatures hath discovered, and number them with those who have circled round Thee, and who move about Thy throne in every world of Thy worlds. Thou, truly, art the Almighty, the All-Knowing, the All-Informed —Bahá'u'lláh

THE FAST

Bahá'u'lláh states in the Kitáb-i-Aqdas:

"We have commanded you to pray and fast from the beginning of maturity [15 years]; this is ordained by God, your Lord and the Lord of your forefathers...

The traveler, the ailing, those who are with child or giving suck, [those who are over 70] are not bound by the Fast... Abstain from food and drink from sunrise to sundown, and beware lest desire deprive you of this grace that is appointed in the Book." [1]

Praise be to Thee, O Lord my God! I beseech Thee by this Revelation whereby darkness hath been turned into light, through which the Frequented Fane hath been built, and the Written Tablet revealed, and the Outspread Roll uncovered, to send down upon me and upon them who are in my company that which will enable us to soar into the heavens of Thy transcendent glory, and will wash us from the stain of such doubts as have hindered the suspicious from entering into the tabernacle of Thy unity.

---

[1] The Fast falls during the month of Ala. Refer to the Badí' Calendar for the exact date.

I am the one, O my Lord, who hath held fast the cord of Thy loving-kindness, and clung to the hem of Thy mercy and favors. Do Thou ordain for me and for my loved ones the good of this world and of the world to come. Supply them, then, with the Hidden Gift Thou didst ordain for the choicest among Thy creatures.

These are, O my Lord, the days in which Thou hast bidden Thy servants to observe the Fast. Blessed is he that observeth the Fast wholly for Thy sake and with absolute detachment from all things except Thee. Assist me and assist them, O my Lord, to obey Thee and to keep Thy precepts. Thou, verily, hast power to do what Thou choosest.

There is no God but Thee, the All-Knowing, the All-Wise. All praise be to God, the Lord of all worlds.

—Bahá'u'lláh

"*...essentially (fasting is) a period of meditation and prayer, of spiritual recuperation, during which the believer must strive to make the necessary readjustments in his inner life, and to refresh and reinvigorate the spiritual forces latent in his soul.*"

—Bahá'u'lláh, Kitáb-i-Aqdas

May be said before breaking fast:

Praise be unto Thee, O Lord my God! We have observed the Fast in conformity with Thy bidding and break it now through Thy love and Thy good-pleasure. Deign to accept, O My God, the deeds that we have performed in Thy path wholly for the sake of Thy beauty with our faces set towards Thy Cause, free from aught else but Thee. Bestow, then, Thy forgiveness upon us, upon our forefathers, and upon all such as have believed in Thee and in Thy mighty signs in this most great, this most glorious Revelation. Potent art Thou to do what Thou choosest. Thou art, verily, the Most Exalted, the Almighty, the Unconstrained. —Bahá'u'lláh

O Divine Providence! As I am abstaining from bodily desires and not occupied with eating and drinking, even so purify and sanctify my heart from the love of anyone save Thyself and shield and protect my soul from corrupt desires and satanic qualities so that my spirit may commune with the breaths of holiness, and fast from the mention of all else besides Thee. —'Abdu'l-Bahá

NAW-RÚZ[1]

He is the Almighty. Praised be Thou, O my God, that Thou hast ordained Naw-Rúz as a festival unto those who have observed the Fast for love of Thee and abstained from all that is abhorrent unto Thee. Grant, O my Lord, that the fire of Thy love and the heat produced by the Fast enjoined by Thee may inflame them in Thy Cause, and make them to be occupied with Thy praise and with remembrance of Thee.

Since Thou hast adorned them, O my Lord, with the ornament of the Fast prescribed by Thee, do Thou adorn them also with the ornament of Thine acceptance, through Thy grace and bountiful favor. For the doings of men are all dependent upon Thy good-pleasure, and are conditioned by Thy behest.

Shouldst Thou regard him who hath broken the Fast as one who hath observed it, such a man would be reckoned among them who from eternity had been keeping the Fast. And shouldst Thou decree that he who hath observed the Fast hath broken it, that person would be numbered with such as have

---

1 Naw-Rúz, is the first day of the Bahá'í year. Refer to the Badí' Calendar for the exact date.

caused the Robe of Thy Revelation to be stained with dust, and been far removed from the crystal waters of this living Fountain.

Thou art He through Whom the ensign "Praiseworthy art Thou in Thy works" hath been lifted up, and the standard "Obeyed art Thou in Thy behest" hath been unfurled. Make known this Thy station, O my God, unto Thy servants, that they may be made aware that the excellence of all things is dependent upon Thy bidding and Thy word, and the virtue of every act is conditioned by Thy leave and the good-pleasure of Thy will, and may recognize that the reins of men's doings are within the grasp of Thine acceptance and Thy commandment.

Make this known unto them, that nothing whatsoever may shut them out from Thy Beauty, in these days whereon the Christ exclaimeth: "All dominion is Thine, O Thou the Begetter of the Spirit (Jesus)!" and Thy Friend (Muhammad) crieth out: "Glory be to Thee, O Thou the Best-Beloved, for that Thou hast uncovered Thy Beauty, and written down for Thy chosen ones what will cause them to attain unto the seat of the revelation of Thy Most

Great Name, through which all the peoples have lamented except such as have detached themselves from all else except Thee, and set themselves towards Him Who is the Revealer of Thyself and the Manifestation of Thine attributes."

He Who is Thy Branch and all Thy company, O my Lord, have broken this day their fast, after having observed it within the precincts of Thy court, and in their eagerness to please Thee. Do Thou ordain for Him, and for them, and for all such as have entered Thy presence in those days all the good Thou didst destine in Thy Book. Supply them, then, with that which will profit them, in both this life and the life beyond. Thou, in truth, art the All-Knowing, the All-Wise.

—Bahá'u'lláh

"The Naw-Rúz Feast should be held on March 21 before sunset and has nothing to do with the Nineteen Day Feast. The Nineteen Day Feast is administrative in function whereas the Naw-Rúz is our New Year, a Feast of hospitality and rejoicing."

—From letter written on behalf of Shoghi Effendi

THE RIḌVÁN TABLET
EXCERPTS

Revealed by Bahá'u'lláh on the 9th Day of Riḍván, in commemoration of the twelve days He spent in the Garden of Riḍván, Baghdad in 1863, and where he declared His Mission

The Divine Springtime is come, O Most Exalted Pen, for the Festival of the All-Merciful is fast approaching. Bestir thyself, and magnify, before the entire creation, the name of God, and celebrate His praise, in such wise that all created things may be regenerated and made new. Speak, and hold not thy peace. The day star of blissfulness shineth above the horizon of Our name, the Blissful, inasmuch as the kingdom of the name of God hath been adorned with the ornament of the name of thy Lord, the Creator of the heavens. Arise before the nations of the earth, and arm thyself with the power of this Most Great Name, and be not of those who tarry...

This is the Day whereon the unseen world crieth out: "Great is thy blessedness, O earth, for thou hast been made the foot-stool of thy God, and been chosen as the seat of His mighty throne." The realm of glory exclaimeth: "Would that my life could be sacrificed for thee, for He Who is the Beloved of the All-Merciful hath established His sovereignty upon thee, through the power of His Name that hath been promised unto all things, whether of the past or of the future..."

Arise, and proclaim unto the entire creation the tidings that He Who is the All-Merciful hath directed His steps towards the Riḍván and entered it. Guide, then, the people unto the garden of delight which God hath made the Throne of His Paradise. We have chosen thee to be our most mighty Trumpet, whose blast is to signalize the resurrection of all mankind.

Attract the hearts of men, through the call of Him, the one alone Beloved. Say: This is the Voice of God, if ye do but hearken. This is the Day Spring of the Revelation of God, did ye but know it. This is the Dawning-Place of the Cause of God, were ye to recognize it. This is the Source of the commandment of God, did ye but judge it fairly. This is the manifest and hidden Secret; would that ye might perceive it. O peoples of the world! Cast away, in My name that transcendeth all other names, the things ye possess, and immerse yourselves in this Ocean in whose depths lay hidden the pearls of wisdom and of utterance, an ocean that surgeth in My name, the All-Merciful. Thus instructeth you He with Whom is the Mother Book.

The Best-Beloved is come. In His right hand is the sealed Wine of His name. Happy is the man that turneth unto Him, and drinketh his fill, and exclaimeth: "Praise be to Thee, O Revealer of the signs of God!" By the righteousness of the Almighty! Every hidden thing hath been manifested through the power of truth. All the favors of God have been sent down, as a token of His grace. The waters of everlasting life have, in their fullness, been proffered unto men. Every single cup hath been borne round by the hand of the Well-Beloved. Draw near, and tarry not, though it be for one short moment...

Rejoice with exceeding gladness, O people of Bahá, as ye call to remembrance the Day of supreme felicity, the Day whereon the Tongue of the Ancient of Days hath spoken, as He departed from His House, proceeding to the Spot from which He shed upon the whole of creation the splendors of His name, the All-Merciful. God is Our witness... —Bahá'u'lláh

TABLET OF AHMAD

He is the King, the All-Knowing, the Wise! Lo, the Nightingale of Paradise singeth upon the twigs of the Tree of Eternity, with holy and sweet melodies, proclaiming to the sincere ones the glad tidings of the nearness of God, calling the believers in the Divine Unity to the court of the Presence of the Generous One, informing the severed ones of the message which hath been revealed by God, the King, the Glorious, the Peerless, guiding the lovers to the seat of sanctity and to this resplendent Beauty.

Verily this is that Most Great Beauty, foretold in the Books of the Messengers, through Whom truth shall be distinguished from error and the wisdom of every command shall be tested. Verily He is the Tree of Life that bringeth forth the fruits of God, the Exalted, the Powerful, the Great.

O Ahmad! Bear thou witness that verily He is God and there is no God but Him, the King, the Protector, the Incomparable, the Omnipotent. And that the One Whom He hath sent forth by the name of 'Alí was the true One from God, to Whose commands we are all conforming.

Say: O people be obedient to the ordinances of God, which have been enjoined in the Bayán by the Glorious, the Wise One. Verily He is the King of the Messengers and His book is the Mother Book did ye but know.

Thus doth the Nightingale utter His call unto you from this prison. He hath but to deliver this clear message. Whosoever desireth, let him turn aside from this counsel and whosoever desireth let him choose the path to his Lord.

O people, if ye deny these verses, by what proof have ye believed in God? Produce it, O assemblage of false ones. Nay, by the One in Whose hand is my soul, they are not, and never shall be able to do this, even should they combine to assist one another.

O Ahmad! Forget not My bounties while I am absent. Remember My days during thy days, and My distress and banishment in this remote prison. And be thou so steadfast in My love that thy heart shall not waver, even if the swords of the enemies rain blows upon thee and all the heavens and the earth arise against thee.

Be thou as a flame of fire to My enemies and a river of life eternal to My loved ones, and be not of those who doubt. And if thou art overtaken by affliction in My path, or degradation for My sake, be not thou troubled thereby.

Rely upon God, thy God and the Lord of thy fathers. For the people are wandering in the paths of delusion, bereft of discernment to see God with their own eyes, or hear His Melody with their own ears. Thus have We found them, as thou also dost witness.

Thus have their superstitions become veils between them and their own hearts and kept them from the path of God, the Exalted, the Great.

Be thou assured in thyself that verily, he who turneth away from this Beauty hath also turned away from the Messengers of the past and showeth pride towards God from all eternity to all eternity.

Learn well this Tablet, O Ahmad. Chant it during thy days and withhold not thyself therefrom.

For verily, God hath ordained for the one who chanteth it, the reward of a hundred martyrs and a service in both worlds. These favors have We bestowed upon thee as a bounty on Our part and a mercy from Our presence, that thou mayest be of those who are grateful.

By God! Should one who is in affliction or grief read this Tablet with absolute sincerity, God will dispel his sadness, solve his difficulties and remove his afflictions.

Verily, He is the Merciful, the Compassionate. Praise be to God, the Lord of all the worlds.

—Bahá'u'lláh

"True remembrance is to make mention of the Lord, the All-Praised, and forget aught else beside Him....

The essence of faith is fewness of words and abundance of deeds; he whose words exceed his deeds, know verily his death is better than his life." —Bahá'u'lláh

FIRE TABLET

Tablet revealed by Bahá'u'lláh Entitled 'Qad Ihtaraqa'l-Mukhlisun'

In the Name of God, the Most Ancient, the Most Great.

Indeed the hearts of the sincere are consumed in the fire of separation:

Where is the gleaming of the light of Thy
Countenance, O Beloved of the worlds?

Those who are near unto Thee have been abandoned in the darkness of desolation:

Where is the shining of the morn of Thy
reunion, O Desire of the worlds?

The bodies of Thy chosen ones lie quivering on distant sands:

Where is the ocean of Thy presence,
O Enchanter of the worlds?

Longing hands are uplifted to the heaven of Thy grace and generosity:

Where are the rains of Thy bestowal,
O Answerer of the worlds?

The infidels have arisen in tyranny on every hand:
Where is the compelling power of Thine ordaining pen, O Conqueror of the worlds?

The barking of dogs is loud on every side:
Where is the lion of the forest of Thy might,
O Chastiser of the worlds?

Coldness hath gripped all mankind:
Where is the warmth of Thy love,
O Fire of the worlds?

Calamity hath reached its height:
Where are the signs of Thy succor,
O Salvation of the worlds?

Darkness hath enveloped most of the peoples:
Where is the brightness of Thy splendor,
O Radiance of the worlds?

The necks of men are stretched out in malice:
Where are the swords of Thy vengeance,
O Destroyer of the worlds?

Abasement hath reached its lowest depth:
Where are the emblems of Thy glory,
O Glory of the worlds?

Sorrows have afflicted the Revealer of Thy Name, the All-Merciful:
Where is the joy of the Dayspring of Thy Revelation, O Delight of the worlds?

Anguish hath befallen all the peoples of the earth:
Where are the ensigns of Thy gladness,
O Joy of the worlds?

Thou seest the Dawning Place of Thy signs veiled by evil suggestions:
Where are the fingers of Thy might,
O Power of the worlds?

Sore thirst hath overcome all men:
Where is the river of Thy bounty,
O Mercy of the worlds?

Greed hath made captive all mankind:
Where are the embodiments of detachment,
O Lord of the worlds?

Thou seest this Wronged One lonely in exile:
Where are the hosts of the heaven of Thy Command, O Sovereign of the worlds?

I have been forsaken in a foreign land:
Where are the emblems of Thy faithfulness,
O Trust of the worlds?

The agonies of death have laid hold on all men:
Where is the surging of Thine ocean of eternal life, O Life of the worlds?

The whisperings of Satan have been breathed to every creature:
Where is the meteor of Thy fire,
O Light of the worlds?

The drunkenness of passion hath perverted most of mankind:
Where are the daysprings of purity,
O Desire of the worlds?

Thou seest this Wronged One veiled in tyranny among the Syrians:
Where is the radiance of Thy dawning light,
O Light of the worlds?

Thou seest Me forbidden to speak forth:
Then from where will spring Thy melodies,
O Nightingale of the worlds?

Most of the people are enwrapped in fancy and idle imaginings:
Where are the exponents of Thy certitude,
O Assurance of the worlds?

Bahá is drowning in a sea of tribulation:
Where is the Ark of Thy salvation,
O Savior of the worlds?

Thou seest the Dayspring of Thine utterance in the darkness of creation:
Where is the sun of the heaven of Thy grace,
O Light-giver of the worlds?

The lamps of truth and purity, of loyalty and honor, have been put out:
Where are the signs of Thine avenging wrath,
O Mover of the Worlds?

Canst Thou see any who have championed Thy Self, or who ponder on what hath befallen Him in the pathway of Thy love?
Now doth My pen halt,
O Beloved of the worlds.

The branches of the Divine Lote-Tree lie broken by the onrushing gales of destiny:
Where are the banners of Thy succor,
O Champion of the worlds?

This Face is hidden in the dust of slander:
Where are the breezes of Thy compassion,
O Mercy of the worlds?

The robe of sanctity is sullied by the people of deceit:
Where is the vesture of Thy holiness,
O Adorner of the worlds?

The sea of grace is stilled for what the hands of men have wrought:
Where are the waves of Thy bounty,
O Desire of the worlds?

The door leading to the Divine Presence is locked through the tyranny of Thy foes:
Where is the key of Thy bestowal,
O Unlocker of the worlds?

The leaves are yellowed by the poisoning winds of sedition:
Where is the downpour of the clouds of Thy bounty, O Giver of the worlds?

The universe is darkened with the dust of sin:
Where are the breezes of Thy forgiveness,
O Forgiver of the worlds?

This Youth is lonely in a desolate land:
Where is the rain of Thy heavenly grace,
O Bestower of the worlds?

O Supreme Pen, We have heard Thy most sweet call in the eternal realm:
    Give Thou ear unto what the Tongue of Grandeur uttereth, O Wronged One of the worlds!

Were it not for the cold,
    how would the heat of Thy words prevail,
    O Expounder of the worlds?

Were it not for calamity,
    how would the sun of Thy patience shine,
    O Light of the worlds?

Lament not because of the wicked.
    Thou wert created to bear and endure,
    O Patience of the worlds.

How sweet was Thy dawning on the horizon of the Covenant among the stirrers of sedition, and
    Thy yearning after God,
    O Love of the worlds.

By Thee the banner of independence was planted on the highest peaks,
    and the sea of bounty surged,
    O Rapture of the worlds.

By Thine aloneness the Sun of Oneness shone,
and by Thy banishment the land of Unity was adorned. Be patient,
O Thou Exile of the worlds.

We have made abasement the garment of glory,
and affliction the adornment of Thy temple,
O Pride of the worlds.

Thou seest the hearts are filled with hate,
and to overlook is Thine,
O Thou Concealer of the sins of the worlds.

When the swords flash, go forward!
When the shafts fly, press onward!
O Thou Sacrifice of the worlds.

Dost Thou wail, or shall I wail? Rather shall I weep
at the fewness of Thy champions,
O Thou Who hast caused the wailing of the worlds.

Verily, I have heard Thy call, O All-Glorious Beloved; and now is the face of Bahá flaming with the heat of tribulation and with the fire of Thy shining word, and He hath risen up in faithfulness at the place of sacrifice, looking toward Thy pleasure,

O Ordainer of the worlds.

O 'Alí-Akbar, thank thy Lord for this Tablet whence thou canst breathe the fragrance of My meekness, and know what hath beset Us in the path of God, the Adored of all the worlds.

Should all the servants read and ponder this, there shall be kindled in their veins a fire that shall set aflame the worlds.

—Bahá'u'lláh

"The mind and spirit of man advance when he is tried by suffering. The more the ground is ploughed the better the seed will grow, the better the harvest will be. Just as the plough furrows the earth deeply, purifying it of weeds and thistles, so suffering and tribulation free man from the petty affairs of this worldly life until he arrives at a state of complete detachment."

—'Abdu'l-Bahá

SPECIAL TABLETS

TABLET OF VISITATION OF BAHÁ'U'LLÁH

This Tablet is read at the Shrine of Bahá'u'lláh and the Shrine of the Báb. It is also frequently used in commemorating Their anniversaries.

The praise which hath dawned from Thy most august Self, and the glory which hath shone forth from Thy most effulgent Beauty, rest upon Thee, O Thou Who art the Manifestation of Grandeur, and the King of Eternity, and the Lord of all who are in heaven and on earth!

I testify that through Thee the sovereignty of God and His dominion, and the majesty of God and His grandeur, were revealed, and the Daystars of ancient splendor have shed their radiance in the heaven of Thine irrevocable decree, and the Beauty of the Unseen hath shone forth above the horizon of creation.

I testify, moreover, that with but a movement of Thy Pen Thine injunction "Be Thou" hath been enforced, and God's hidden Secret hath been divulged, and all created things have been called into being, and all the Revelations have been sent down.

I bear witness, moreover, that through Thy beauty the beauty of the Adored One hath been unveiled, and through Thy face the face of the Desired One hath shone forth, and that through a word from Thee Thou hast decided between all created things, causing them who are devoted to Thee to ascend unto the summit of glory, and the infidels to fall into the lowest abyss.

I bear witness that he who hath known Thee hath known God, and he who hath attained unto Thy presence hath attained unto the presence of God. Great, therefore, is the blessedness of him who hath believed in Thee, and in Thy signs, and hath humbled himself before Thy sovereignty, and hath been honored with meeting Thee, and hath attained the good pleasure of Thy will, and circled around Thee, and stood before Thy throne.

Woe betide him that hath transgressed against Thee, and hath denied Thee, and repudiated Thy signs, and gainsaid Thy sovereignty, and risen up against Thee, and waxed proud before Thy face, and hath disputed Thy testimonies, and fled from Thy rule and Thy dominion, and been numbered with the infidels whose names have been inscribed by the fingers of Thy behest upon Thy holy Tablets.

Waft, then, unto me, O my God and my Beloved, from the right hand of Thy mercy and Thy loving-kindness, the holy breaths of Thy favors, that they may draw me away from myself and from the world unto the courts of Thy nearness and Thy presence. Potent art Thou to do what pleaseth Thee. Thou, truly, hast been supreme over all things.

The remembrance of God and His praise, and the glory of God and His splendor, rest upon Thee, O Thou Who art His Beauty! I bear witness that the eye of creation hath never gazed upon one wronged like Thee. Thou wast immersed all the days of Thy life beneath an ocean of tribulations. At one time Thou wast in chains and fetters; at another Thou wast threatened by the sword of Thine enemies. Yet, despite all this, Thou didst enjoin upon all men to observe what had been prescribed unto Thee by Him Who is the All-Knowing, the All-Wise.

May my spirit be a sacrifice to the wrongs Thou didst suffer, and my soul be a ransom for the adversities Thou didst sustain. I beseech God, by Thee and by them whose faces have been illumined with the splendors of the light of Thy countenance, and who, for love of Thee, have observed all whereunto they were bidden, to remove the veils that have come in between Thee and Thy creatures, and to supply me with the good of this world and the world to come. Thou art, in truth, the Almighty, the Most Exalted, the All-Glorious, the Ever-Forgiving, the Most Compassionate.

Bless Thou, O Lord my God, the Divine Lote-Tree and its leaves, and its boughs, and its branches, and its stems, and its offshoots, as long as Thy most excellent titles will endure and Thy most august attributes will last. Protect it, then, from the mischief of the aggressor and the hosts of tyranny. Thou art, in truth, the Almighty, the Most Powerful.

Bless Thou, also, O Lord my God, Thy servants and Thy handmaidens who have attained unto Thee. Thou, truly, art the All-Bountiful, Whose grace is infinite. No God is there save Thee, the Ever-Forgiving, the Most Generous. —Bahá'u'lláh

PRAYER OF VISITATION OF 'ABDU'L-BAHÁ

This prayer, revealed by 'Abdu'l-Bahá, is read at His Shrine. It is also used in private prayer.

Whoso reciteth this prayer with lowliness and fervor will bring gladness and joy to the heart of this Servant; it will be even as meeting Him face to face.

He is the All-Glorious! O God, my God! Lowly and tearful, I raise my suppliant hands to Thee and cover my face in the dust of that Threshold of Thine, exalted above the knowledge of the learned, and the praise of all that glorify Thee. Graciously look upon Thy servant, humble and lowly at Thy door, with the glances of the eye of Thy mercy, and immerse him in the Ocean of Thine eternal grace.

Lord! He is a poor and lowly servant of Thine, enthralled and imploring Thee, captive in Thy hand, praying fervently to Thee, trusting in Thee, in tears before Thy face, calling to Thee and beseeching Thee, saying:

O Lord, my God! Give me Thy grace to serve Thy loved ones, strengthen me in my servitude to Thee, illumine my brow with the light of adoration in Thy court of holiness, and of prayer to Thy kingdom of grandeur. Help me to be selfless at the heavenly entrance of Thy gate, and aid me to be detached from all things within Thy holy precincts. Lord! Give me to drink from the chalice of selflessness; with its robe clothe me, and in its ocean immerse me. Make me as dust in the pathway of Thy loved ones, and grant that I may offer up my soul for the earth ennobled by the footsteps of Thy chosen ones in Thy path, O Lord of Glory in the Highest.

With this prayer doth Thy servant call Thee, at dawntide and in the night-season. Fulfill his heart's desire, O Lord! Illumine his heart, gladden his bosom, kindle his light, that he may serve Thy Cause and Thy-servants.

Thou art the Bestower, the Pitiful, the Most Bountiful, the Gracious, the Merciful, the Compassionate.

—'Abdu'l-Bahá

PRAYER TO BE SAID WHEN VISITING NAVVAB'S RESTING PLACE

O faithful ones! Should ye visit the resting-place of the Most Exalted Leaf (Navvab) who hath ascended unto the Glorious Companion, stand ye and say:

Salutation and blessing and glory upon thee, O Holy Leaf that hath sprung from the Divine Lote-Tree! I bear witness that thou hast believed in God and in His signs, and answered His Call, and turned unto Him, and held fast unto His cord, and clung to the hem of His grace, and fled thy home in His path, and chosen to live as a stranger, out of love for His presence and in thy longing to serve Him.

May God have mercy upon him that draweth nigh unto thee, and remembereth thee through the things which My Pen hath voiced in this, the most great station. We pray God that He may forgive us, and forgive them that have turned unto thee, and grant their desires, and bestow upon them, through His wondrous grace, whatever be their wish. He, verily, is the Bountiful, the Generous. Praise be to God, He Who is the Desire of all worlds; and the Beloved of all who recognize Him. —Bahá'u'lláh

SELECTED HOLY WRITINGS

HIDDEN WORDS OF BAHÁ'U'LLÁH
- A SELECTION -

O SON OF SPIRIT!

My first counsel is this: Possess a pure, kindly and radiant heart, that thine may be a sovereignty ancient, imperishable and everlasting

O SON OF SPIRIT!

The best beloved of all things in My sight is Justice; turn not away therefrom if thou desirest Me, and neglect it not that I may confide in thee. By its aid thou shalt see with thine own eyes and not through the eyes of others, and shalt know of thine own knowledge and not through the knowledge of thy neighbor. Ponder this in thy heart; how it behooveth thee to be. Verily justice is My gift to thee and the sign of My loving-kindness. Set it then before thine eyes.

O SON OF MAN!

Veiled in My immemorial being and in the ancient eternity of My essence, I knew My love for thee; therefore I created thee, have engraved on thee Mine image and revealed to thee My beauty.

O SON OF BEING!

Love Me, that I may love thee. If thou lovest Me not, My love can in no wise reach thee. Know this, O servant.

O SON OF BEING!

Thy Paradise is My love; thy heavenly home, reunion with Me. Enter therein and tarry not. This is that which hath been destined for thee in Our kingdom above and Our exalted dominion.

O SON OF SPIRIT!

Ask not of Me that which We desire not for thee, then be content with what We have ordained for thy sake, for this is that which profiteth thee, if therewith thou dost content thyself.

O SON OF SPIRIT!

Noble have I created thee, yet thou hast abased thyself. Rise then unto that for which thou wast created.

O SON OF MAN!

Breathe not the sins of others so long as thou art thyself a sinner. Shouldst thou transgress this command, accursed wouldst thou be, and to this I bear witness.

O SON OF BEING!

Bring thyself to account each day ere thou art summoned to a reckoning; for death, unheralded, shall come upon thee and thou shalt be called to give account for thy deeds.

O SON OF SPIRIT!

With the joyful tidings of light I hail thee: rejoice! To the court of holiness I summon thee; abide therein that thou mayest live in peace forevermore.

O SON OF MAN!

Neglect not My commandments if thou lovest My beauty, and forget not My counsels if thou wouldst attain My good pleasure.

O SON OF MAN!

Humble thyself before Me, that I may graciously visit thee. Arise for the triumph of My cause, that while yet on earth thou mayest obtain the victory.

O SON OF MAN!

For everything there is a sign. The sign of love is fortitude under My decree and patience under My trials.

O SON OF MAN!

Should prosperity befall thee, rejoice not, and should abasement come upon thee, grieve not, for both shall pass away and be no more.

O YE RICH ONES ON EARTH!

The poor in your midst are My trust; guard ye My trust, and be not intent only on your own ease.

WRITINGS OF BAHÁ'U'LLÁH
- A SELECTION -

The Ancient Beauty hath consented to be bound with chains that mankind may be released from its bondage, and hath accepted to be made a prisoner within this most mighty Stronghold that the whole world may attain unto true liberty.

He hath drained to its dregs the cup of sorrow, that all the peoples of the earth may attain unto abiding joy, and be filled with gladness. This is of the mercy of your Lord, the Compassionate, the Most Merciful. We have accepted to be abased, O believers in the Unity of God, that ye may be exalted, and have suffered manifold afflictions, that ye might prosper and flourish.

He Who hath come to build anew the whole world, behold, how they that have joined partners with God have forced Him to dwell within the most desolate of cities!

—Bahá'u'lláh

O friends! Be not careless of the virtues with which ye have been endowed, neither be neglectful of your high destiny. Suffer not your labors to be wasted through the vain imaginations which certain hearts have devised.

Ye are the stars of the heaven of understanding, the breeze that stirreth at the break of day, the soft-flowing waters upon which must depend the very life of all men, the letters inscribed upon His sacred scroll.

With the utmost unity, and in a spirit of perfect fellowship, exert yourselves, that ye may be enabled to achieve that which beseemeth this Day of God.

Verily I say, strife and dissension, and whatsoever the mind of man abhorreth are entirely unworthy of his station. Center your energies in the propagation of the Faith of God.

—Bahá'u'lláh

Be generous in prosperity, and thankful in adversity. Be worthy of the trust of thy neighbor, and look upon him with a bright and friendly face. Be a treasure to the poor, an admonisher to the rich, an answerer of the cry of the needy, a preserver of the sanctity of thy pledge. Be fair in thy judgment, and guarded in thy speech. Be unjust to no man, and show all meekness to all men. Be as a lamp unto them that walk in darkness, a joy to the sorrowful, a sea for the thirsty, a haven for the distressed, an upholder and defender of the victim of oppression.

Let integrity and uprightness distinguish all thine acts. Be a home for the stranger, a balm to the suffering, a tower of strength for the fugitive. Be eyes to the blind, and a guiding light unto the feet of the erring. Be an ornament to the countenance of truth,

a crown to the brow of fidelity,
a pillar of the temple of righteousness,
a breath of life to the body of mankind,
an ensign of the hosts of justice,
a luminary above the horizon of virtue,
a dew to the soil of the human heart,
an ark on the ocean of knowledge,
a sun in the heaven of bounty,
a gem on the diadem of wisdom,
a shining light in the firmament of thy generation,
a fruit upon the tree of humility. —Bahá'u'lláh

WRITINGS OF 'ABDU'L-BAHÁ
- A SELECTION -

O thou who art turning thy face towards God! Close thine eyes to all things else,and open them to the realm of the All-Glorious.

Ask whatsoever thou wishest of Him alone; seek whatsoever thou seekest from Him alone. With a look He granteth a hundred thousand hopes, with a glance He healeth a hundred thousand incurable ills, with a nod He layeth balm on every wound, with a glimpse He freeth the hearts from the shackles of grief.

He doeth as He doeth, and what recourse have we? He carrieth out His Will, He ordaineth what He pleaseth. Then better for thee to bow down thy head in submission, and put thy trust in the All-Merciful Lord. —'Abdu'l-Bahá

My name is 'Abdu'l-Bahá, my identity is 'Abdu'l-Bahá, my qualification is 'Abdu'l-Bahá, my reality is 'Abdu'l-Bahá, my praise is 'Abdu'l-Bahá. Thraldom to the Blessed Perfection is my glorious and refulgent diadem; and servitude to all the human race is my perpetual religion... No name, no title, no mention, no commendation hath he nor will ever have except 'Abdu'l-Bahá. This is my longing. This is my supreme apex. This is my greatest yearning. This is my eternal life . This is my everlasting glory!

—'Abdu'l-Bahá

Beg everything thou desirest from Bahá'u'lláh If thou art asking faith, ask of Him. If thou art yearning after knowledge, He will grant it unto thee. If thou art longing for the love of God, He will bestow it upon thee. He will descend upon thee all His blessings.

—'Abdu'l-Bahá

PRAYER FOR MAKING A DIFFICULT DECISION

This prayer was revealed for Jináb-i-Samandar (Shaykh Kázim Samandar), the father of the Hand of the Cause of God: Tarázu'lláh Samandarí, to assist him in making a difficult decision.

"*In regard to his affairs, let him repeat nineteen times:*

O my God! Thou seest me detached from everything save Thee and clinging to Thee.

Guide me then, in my doings, in a manner which profiteth me for the glory of Thy Cause and the loftiness of the state of Thy servants.

Let him then reflect upon the matter & undertake whatever cometh to mind." —Bahá'u'lláh

DYNAMICS OF PRAYER FOR SOLVING PROBLEMS

Step 1: Pray and meditate about it. Use the prayers of the Manifestations as they have the greatest power. Then remain in the silence of contemplation for a few minutes.

Step 2: Arrive at a decision and hold this. This decision is usually born during the contemplation. It may seem almost impossible of accomplishment but if it seems to be as answer to a prayer or a way of solving the problem, then immediately take the next step.

Step 3: Have determination to carry the decision through. Many fail here. The decision, budding into determination, is blighted and instead becomes a wish or a vague longing. When determination is born, immediately take the next step.

Step 4: Have faith and confidence that the power will flow through you, the right way will appear, the door will open, the right thought, the right message, the right principle or the right book will be given you. Have confidence, and the right thing will come to your need. Then, as you rise from prayer, take at once the fifth step.

Step 5: Act as though it had all been answered. Then act with tireless, ceaseless energy. And as you act, you, yourself, will become a magnet, which will attract more power to your being, until you become an unobstructed channel for the Divine power to flow through you.

Many pray but do not remain for the last half of the first step. Some who meditate arrive at a decision, but fail to hold it. Few have the determination to carry the decision through, still fewer have the confidence that the right thing will come to their need. But how many remember to act as though it had all been answered? How true are these words— "Greater than the prayer is the spirit in which it is uttered" and greater than the way it is uttered is the spirit in which it is carried out.

These steps were suggested by Shoghi Effendi to a believer as a method of finding a solution to problems using prayer.

-Shoghi Effendi, Principles of Bahá'í Administration pg.90

NINETEEN DAY FEAST

O God! Dispel all those elements which are the cause of discord, and prepare for us all those things which are the cause of unity and accord! O God! Descend upon us Heavenly Fragrance and change this gathering into a gathering of Heaven! Grant to us every benefit and every food. Prepare for us the Food of Love! Give to us the Food of Knowledge! Bestow upon us the Food of Heavenly Illumination!

— 'Abdu'l-Bahá

"The adoption of a new calendar in each dispensation is a symbol of the power of Divine Revelation to reshape human perception of material, social, and spiritual reality. Through it, sacred moments are distinguished, humanity's place in time and space reimagined, and the rhythm of life recast. Next Naw-Rúz (2015) will mark yet another historic step in the manifestation of the unity of the people of Bahá and the unfoldment of Bahá'u'lláh's World Order."

—The Universal House of Justice

THE BADÍ` CALENDAR

The Bahá'í' Era (BE) began with the Declaration of the Báb in 1844. The Báb introduced the Badí' Calendar. Bahá'u'lláh provided essential clarifications and additions. Badí' means "to create a-new" as well as "wondrous" and "unique".

The Bahá'í' New Year, Naw-Rúz, is astronomically fixed commencing at the March equinox, (20th or 21st March), consisting of 19 months of 19 days each (i.e. 361 days) with the addition of certain 'Intercalary Days' (4 in ordinary year and 5 in leap year) between the 18th and 19th months in order to adjust the calendar to the solar year.

Each day begins and ends at sunset. Each month and the days of a month as well as the days of a week are named after attributes of God.

Each period of 19 years is called a "Váhid" and 19 Váhids comprise a "Kull-i-Shay" (361 years). March 20th 2015 signalized the end of year 171 and the close of the 9th Váhid of the first Kull-i-Shay of the Bahá'í' Era.

BAHÁ'Í DATES 175 TO 186 B.E.

Dates of Naw-Rúz, the Twin Holy Birthdays, and Ayyám-i-Há

Naw-Rúz		The Birth of the Báb & The Birth of Bahá'u'lláh		Ayyám-i-Há	
1 Bahá 175	21 Mar 2018	6, 7 Qudrat	9, 10 Nov 2018	1–4	26 Feb–1 Mar 2019
1 Bahá 176	21 Mar 2019	14, 15 'Ilm	29, 30 Oct 2019	1–4	26–29 Feb 2020
1 Bahá 177	20 Mar 2020	4, 5 'Ilm	18, 19 Oct 2020	1–4	25–28 Feb 2021
1 Bahá 178	20 Mar 2021	4, 5 Qudrat	6, 7 Nov 2021	1–5	25 Feb–1 Mar 2022
1 Bahá 179	21 Mar 2022	11, 12 'Ilm	26, 27 Oct 2022	1–4	26 Feb–1 Mar 2023
1 Bahá 180	21 Mar 2023	1, 2 'Ilm	16, 17 Oct 2023	1–4	26–29 Feb 2024
1 Bahá 181	20 Mar 2024	19 'Ilm, 1 Qudrat	2, 3 Nov 2024	1–4	25–28 Feb 2025
1 Bahá 182	20 Mar 2025	8, 9 'Ilm	22, 23 Oct 2025	1–5	25 Feb–1 Mar 2026
1 Bahá 183	21 Mar 2026	7, 8 Qudrat	10, 11 Nov 2026	1–4	26 Feb–1 Mar 2027
1 Bahá 184	21 Mar 2027	15, 16 'Ilm	30, 31 Oct 2027	1–4	26–29 Feb 2028
1 Bahá 185	20 Mar 2028	5, 6 'Ilm	19, 20 Oct 2028	1–4	25–28 Feb 2029
1 Bahá 186	20 Mar 2029	5, 6 Qudrat	7, 8 Nov 2029	1–4	25–28 Feb 2030

Note: The Bahá'í day ends and a new one begins at sunset; consequently, the day on which a Feast or Holy Day is observed begins at sunset of the day before the Gregorian calendar dates given above.

BAHÁ'Í DATES 187 TO 198 B.E.

Dates of Naw-Rúz, the Twin Holy Birthdays, and Ayyám-i-Há

Naw-Rúz		The Birth of the Báb & The Birth of Bahá'u'lláh		Ayyám-i-Há	
1 Bahá 187	20 Mar 2030	14, 15 'Ilm	28, 29 Oct 2030	1–5	25 Feb–1 Mar 2031
1 Bahá 188	21 Mar 2031	2, 3 'Ilm	17, 18 Oct 2031	1–4	26–29 Feb 2032
1 Bahá 189	20 Mar 2032	2, 3 Qudrat	4, 5 Nov 2032	1–4	25–28 Feb 2033
1 Bahá 190	20 Mar 2033	10, 11 'Ilm	24, 25 Oct 2033	1–4	25–28 Feb 2034
1 Bahá 191	20 Mar 2034	10, 11 Qudrat	12, 13 Nov 2034	1–5	25 Feb–1 Mar 2035
1 Bahá 192	21 Mar 2035	17, 18 'Ilm	1, 2 Nov 2035	1–4	26–29 Feb 2036
1 Bahá 193	20 Mar 2036	6, 7 'Ilm	20, 21 Oct 2036	1–4	25–28 Feb 2037
1 Bahá 194	20 Mar 2037	6, 7 Qudrat	8, 9 Nov 2037	1–4	25–28 Feb 2038
1 Bahá 195	20 Mar 2038	15, 16 'Ilm	29, 30 Oct 2038	1–5	25 Feb–1 Mar 2039
1 Bahá 196	21 Mar 2039	4, 5 'Ilm	19, 20 Oct 2039	1–4	26–29 Feb 2040
1 Bahá 197	20 Mar 2040	4, 5 Qudrat	6, 7 Nov 2040	1–4	25–28 Feb 2041
1 Bahá 198	20 Mar 2041	12, 13 'Ilm	26, 27 Oct 2041	1–4	25–28 Feb 2042

Dates of Naw-Rúz, the Twin Holy Birthdays, and Ayyám-i-Há

Naw-Rúz		The Birth of the Báb & The Birth of Bahá'u'lláh		Ayyám-i-Há	
1 Bahá 199	20 Mar 2042	1, 2 'Ilm	15, 16 Oct 2042	1-5	25 Feb-1 Mar 2043
1 Bahá 200	21 Mar 2043	19 'Ilm, 1 Qudrat	3, 4 Nov 2043	1-4	26-29 Feb 2044
1 Bahá 201	20 Mar 2044	8, 9 'Ilm	22, 23 Oct 2044	1-4	25-28 Feb 2045
1 Bahá 202	20 Mar 2045	8, 9 Qudrat	10, 11 Nov 2045	1-4	25-28 Feb 2046
1 Bahá 203	20 Mar 2046	16, 17 'Ilm	30, 31 Oct 2046	1-5	25 Feb-1 Mar 2047
1 Bahá 204	21 Mar 2047	5, 6 'Ilm	20, 21 Oct 2047	1-4	26-29 Feb 2048
1 Bahá 205	20 Mar 2048	5, 6 Qudrat	7, 8 Nov 2048	1-4	25-28 Feb 2049
1 Bahá 206	20 Mar 2049	14, 15 'Ilm	28, 29 Oct 2049	1-4	25-28 Feb 2050
1 Bahá 207	20 Mar 2050	3, 4 'Ilm	17, 18 Oct 2050	1-5	25 Feb-1 Mar 2051
1 Bahá 208	21 Mar 2051	2, 3 Qudrat	5, 6 Nov 2051	1-4	26-29 Feb 2052
1 Bahá 209	20 Mar 2052	10, 11 'Ilm	24, 25 Oct 2052	1-4	25-28 Feb 2053

BAHÁ'Í DATES 211 TO 221 B.E.

Dates of Naw-Rúz, the Twin Holy Birthdays, and Ayyám-i-Há

Naw-Rúz		The Birth of the Báb & The Birth of Bahá'u'lláh		Ayyám-i-Há	
1 Bahá 211	20 Mar 2054	18, 19 'Ilm	1, 2 Nov 2054	1–5	25 Feb–1 Mar 2055
1 Bahá 212	21 Mar 2055	6, 7 'Ilm	21, 22 Oct 2055	1–4	26–29 Feb 2056
1 Bahá 213	20 Mar 2056	6, 7 Qudrat	8, 9 Nov 2056	1–4	25–28 Feb 2057
1 Bahá 214	20 Mar 2057	15, 16 'Ilm	29, 30 Oct 2057	1–4	25–28 Feb 2058
1 Bahá 215	20 Mar 2058	4, 5 'Ilm	18, 19 Oct 2058	1–4	25–28 Feb 2059
1 Bahá 216	20 Mar 2059	4, 5 Qudrat	6, 7 Nov 2059	1–5	25–29 Feb 2060
1 Bahá 217	20 Mar 2060	11, 12 'Ilm	25, 26 Oct 2060	1–4	25–28 Feb 2061
1 Bahá 218	20 Mar 2061	19 Mashíyyat, 1 'Ilm	14, 15 Oct 2061	1–4	25–28 Feb 2062
1 Bahá 219	20 Mar 2062	19 'Ilm, 1 Qudrat	2, 3 Nov 2062	1–4	25–28 Feb 2063
1 Bahá 220	20 Mar 2063	9, 10 'Ilm	23, 24 Oct 2063	1–5	25–29 Feb 2064
1 Bahá 221	20 Mar 2064	8, 9 Qudrat	10, 11 Nov 2064	1–4	25–28 Feb 2065

OTHER SIGNIFICANT DATES

BAHÁ'Í DATES		GREGORIAN EQUIVALENT	
Other Holy Days		In a year when Naw-Rúz is the same as **20 March**	In a year when Naw-Rúz is the same as **21 March**
First Day of Ridván	13 Jalál	20 April	21 April
Ninth Day of Riḍván	2 Jamál	28 April	29 April
Twelfth Day of Riḍván	5 Jamál	1 May	2 May
Declaration of the Báb	8 'Aẓamat	23 May	24 May
Ascension of Bahá'u'lláh	13 'Aẓamat	28 May	29 May
Martyrdom of the Báb	17 Raḥmat	9 July	10 July
Day of the Covenant	4 Qawl	25 November	26 November
Ascension of 'Abdu'l-Bahá	6 Qawl	27 November	28 November
Feast Days			
Bahá (Splendour)	1 Bahá	20 March	21 March
Jalál (Glory)	1 Jalál	8 April	9 April
Jamál (Beauty)	1 Jamál	27 April	28 April

'Aẓamat (Grandeur)	1 'Aẓamat	16 May	17 May
Núr (Light)	1 Núr	4 June	5 June
Raḥmat (Mercy)	1 Raḥmat	23 June	24 June
Kalimát (Words)	1 Kalimát	12 July	13 July
Kamál (Perfection)	1 Kamál	31 July	1 August
Asmá' (Names)	1 Asmá'	19 August	20 August
'Izzat (Might)	1 'Izzat	7 September	8 September
Mashíyyat (Will)	1 Mashíyyat	26 September	27 September
'Ilm (Knowledge)	1 'Ilm	15 October	16 October
Qudrat (Power)	1 Qudrat	3 November	4 November
Qawl (Speech)	1 Qawl	22 November	23 November
Masá'il (Questions)	1 Masá'il	11 December	12 December
Sharaf (Honour)	1 Sharaf	30 December	31 December
Sulṭán (Sovereignty)	1 Sulṭán	18 January	19 January
Mulk (Dominion)	1 Mulk	6 February	7 February
'Alá' (Loftiness) - The Fast	1 'Alá'	The month of fasting begins when Ayyám-i-Há ends. The dates for Ayyám-i-Há are [illegible] above.	